Living Waters

TOM HARPUR

Living Waters

SELECTED WRITINGS ON SPIRITUALITY

Thomas Allen Publishers

Toronto

Library and Archives Canada Cataloguing in Publication

Harpur, Tom
Living waters : selected writings on spirituality / Tom Harpur.

ISBN-13: 978-0-88762-225-0
ISBN-10: 0-88762-225-9.--

1. Spiritual life.   I. Title.

BL624.H368   2006   204'.4   C2006-900554-0

Editor: Janice Zawerbny
Cover image: Veer

Published by Thomas Allen Publishers,
a division of Thomas Allen & Son Limited,
145 Front Street East, Suite 209,
Toronto, Ontario M5A 1E3 Canada

www.thomas-allen.com

**Canada Council
for the Arts**

The publisher gratefully acknowledges the support of
the Ontario Arts Council for its publishing program.

We acknowledge the support of the Canada Council for the Arts, which
last year invested $21.7 million in writing and publishing throughout Canada.

We acknowledge the support of the Government of Ontario through the
Ontario Media Development Corporation's Ontario Book Initiative.

We acknowledge the financial support of the Government of Canada through the Book
Publishing Industry Development Program (BPIDP) for our publishing activities.

09 08 07 06 05   1 2 3 4 5

Printed and bound in Canada

To all the readers of my books and columns whose
support and enthusiasm have always meant so much

For with you is the fountain of life
and in your light shall we see light.

— PSALM 36:9

CONTENTS

Acknowledgments

———————

Publisher, editor and author have a kind of symbiotic relationship that when it is a natural and harmonious fit can only be described as one of delight. This has been my experience with the leadership at Thomas Allen. My sincere gratitude to Patrick Crean, my publisher, for his vision and constant encouragement, and to Janice Zawerbny, my editor, for her patience, keen critical eye and her ability to remain calm no matter how rough the sea. And, of course, it was Susan's loving devotion to the task that originally transformed these writings from the chaos of a pile of newspaper clippings into a book. My most profound thanks to all of you.

You shall be like a watered garden
like a deep spring whose waters never fail.

— ISAIAH 58:11

Living Waters

INTRODUCTION

THE SPRING OF LIVING WATER

There was once a vast wilderness, void of all vegetation but thorns and brambles. Through the desert wound a highway along which all humankind was making a pilgrimage. People straggled along it, thirsty, tired, and frightened by a host of fears.

But at one point a spring of water bubbled out of the rock. For countless ages the travellers journeying along this road stopped to refresh themselves there. As they did so, they found to their surprise that the waters not only slaked their thirst but satisfied their deeper needs as well. Somehow they found healing and their hopes and courage growing strong again. Life became rich with fresh meaning. They could grasp their various burdens and take to the way again with new hearts. They called the spot "the place of living waters" and the spring itself "the water of life."

As time went on, many began to roll up boulders as monuments of gratitude. As generations passed, these became ever more elaborate until the spring at last was totally enclosed, arched over by a great fortress-like cathedral protected by high walls.

A caste of men, with peculiar robes and a special language, began to set rules for preserving the purity of the well. Access was no longer free, and arguments over who could drink there, when and how often, grew so bitter that wars were fought over them.

The victors always put up more monuments in gratitude for winning, and so it was that, as the years rolled by, the spring was also bricked over and lost from view. But when pilgrims complained and many were found fainting or near death on the road, those in charge mocked their cries or ignored them. Ornate services were carried out within the "holy place" to celebrate what the water had done for pilgrims in the past, while at the gates people died of thirst.

Eventually, other water was piped in, but it seemed a shadow compared with the reality that had once been there for all. Sometimes, strange figures came from the wilderness, saying that the guardians of the well should repent and tear away all obstructions so that the masses might drink. Later, they were called prophets and were honoured greatly. But at the moment of their protest they were rejected. Many were killed. So, in the end, the majority of those who journeyed along avoided the place and survived whatever way they could. Many, recalling the stories they had learned in youth about the spring, were seized with nostalgia and longings too deep to utter. Others struggled on, embittered by doubts that the healing water had ever existed.

Yet, sometimes, at night, when all the ceremonies were stilled, and the lights were out, those few pilgrims who stole into the shrine to rest briefly in some corner were sure they could hear an almost miraculous sound. From somewhere deep under the foundations of that great structure there came the faint echo of running waters. And their eyes would brim with tears. . . .

Some may recognize this "parable," but many will see it here for the first time. The original imagery is as old as the Bible itself. However, this is my own particular version.

What I have come to see and understand in my spiritual journey of late is that the metaphor of the well or of "the fountain of life," to use the words of the Psalmist, refers not to a message or to a gift from "outside," but to an inner reality already present but too often unknown in every heart/mind. This reality is the pearl of great price, the philosopher's stone, the mystery kept secret by hiero-phants of old, the special "gnosis" of the Gnostics, the wisdom of the sages from the dawn of humankind. It is this: that there is deep in the body/mind/spirit reality of every human being a secret spring welling up continuously—it is from a divine, hidden source and is the secret of our true humanity.

What this means is that the ancient metaphor of the spring is still valid and relevant, but I have discovered that its connotation is much more personal than it might seem at first sight. My own path has deepened the realization that the "well of living water" does not lie off beyond us somewhere. It lies within us and awaits us there. Religious institutions and dogmas can indeed block or choke it off. But the greatest impediment comes from ourselves. Others can speak of it or point to it, but only we can discover it and let it flow. Otherwise, to use a Polynesian simile once used by the great mythologist Joseph Campbell, we are like a person standing on the back of a whale while fishing for minnows.

The growing numbers of those who now find themselves on the outside of organized religion have in many cases lost faith in the availability of any "living water," that is, an experience of the divine Mystery. They are fed up with empty dogma and dry, literal depend-ency upon ancient texts or traditions. Still, all evidence strongly sug-gests that people deeply want food and drink for the spirit. Some suspect that it may once have been available, but they can discern it no longer.

This, then, is the meaning of the parable and the underlying theme throughout this book. The essential task for religion in the western world at this moment is to assist humanity in the removal of all blocks and accretions cutting off the "water of life"—the immediate experience of the Living God. Nothing else will satisfy. It is my sincere hope and prayer that this book will play some small part in furthering that goal.

The selections in the first chapter, Surprised by Joy, talk of how we find meaning for our lives, moments in nature and within that surprise and inspire us—as Ralph Waldo Emerson said: "The true mark of genius is to see the miraculous in the common."

Chapter 2, New Horizons for the Journey, challenges the rigid religious thinking of the past and helps us develop a more rational, fulfilling and contemporary faith.

Chapter 3, Our Rituals Have Cosmic Links, shows how our yearly celebrations began in ancient times by observing humanity's "first Bible"—the seasonal cycles and the starry skies above.

Chapter 4, Pearl of Great Price, illuminates our search for a deeper wisdom amidst the distracting chaos of today's world—discovering who we really are.

Chapter 5, Transformation, explores how we may at times be meant to face adversity and learn from it—part of our spiritual metamorphosis as we prepare for our final journey home.

Tom Harpur
Spring 2006

1

SURPRISED BY JOY

You will show me the path of life:
in your presence is fullness of joy.
— PSALM 16:11

SPIRITUAL JOURNEY CAN BE
FULL OF SURPRISES

To follow a spiritual path is to try, with your utmost despite set-backs, to be obedient to the divine within and above yourself. Over the years, there is one thing you learn about this endeavour: it is a journey of great surprises.

Ralph Waldo Emerson, the nineteenth-century American philosopher-poet, reminds us that we often get in our own way here and fail to be surprised because our own expectations of par-ticular results—our belief that we know what it is we are meant to discover—preclude the gift of the unexpected. What we think we want gets in the way of what the Over-Soul (God) is offering. Emerson taught that true discovery is always made obliquely, or at a "slant," as I call it, rather than directly, because of our plans.

He tells us in one essay: "I prefer to say with the old prophet, 'Seekest thou great things? Seek them not.' Life is a boundless priv-ilege, and when you pay for your ticket and get into the car [of a train], you have no guess what good company you shall find there.

You buy much that is not rendered in the bill. Men achieve a certain greatness unawares, when working to another aim. . . ."

The conscious desire and effort to have special moments of insight or inspiration can prevent their occurrence. It's important to be sincerely seeking to know and do the will of God, but without a specific shopping list. Life is a series of surprises. Emerson says we don't guess today "the mood, the pleasure, the power of tomorrow, when we are building up our being." Certainly, with regard to ordinary matters—acts of routine and sense—we can tell somewhat; "but the masterpieces of God, the . . . growths and universal movements of the soul, he hideth."

To be open but to prejudge nothing, Emerson says, is the recipe for new and unexpected knowing. In the Bible's Book of Psalms, my own favourite section of the Scriptures, this patient and obedient approach is called quite simply "waiting upon God." The Quakers, or Society of Friends, as they are called, know all about this. They make it a practice to "wait" upon the inner light. It is another way of imaging the living water within.

Robert Frost echoes this same truth in a poem where he finds himself walking disconsolately through a snow-filled forest one day. Suddenly a bird takes flight, dislodging a flurry of flakes that come glistening down. The moment takes him by surprise and its soul-imprint saves "a day I had rued."

I had a similar experience recently while out with my dog, a yellow Labrador named Buddy. We were hiking through apple orchards and fields—and for no particular reason a sense of melancholy, which we all can experience occasionally, settled around me. The clouds were heavy, with light rain falling, and there was a hint of approaching winter as leaves tumbled in the wind. Wedges of geese passed noisily overhead.

Suddenly I heard the sound of Caribbean voices singing. The sun-drenched lilt of Jamaican accents floated down through the apple-laden trees. Several workers from the distant island were perched high on ladders happily picking fruit and wholly ignoring the weather. As with Robert Frost, my low spirits faded miraculously. The last time I saw these men they were pruning the bare trees while snow fell all around. Now, at full cycle, it was harvest again. I felt strangely stirred, and my soul took sudden flight. Like C. S. Lewis in his book of that name, I was "surprised by joy."

The surprises, however, are not all such little ones, as you travel on. Sometimes they're monumental. That's what has been happening lately in my life. Ever since I first planned to enter seminary years ago, two major concerns have been constants in my mind. One mirrored the other. The first was the deeply painful awareness that religion, in spite of all that can be said (and there is much) in its defence and praise, is almost universally a divisive, disruptive, too often violent element in human affairs. Never mind the rivalries and hostilities between different faiths for a moment. Consider the absurd phenomenon of over four hundred different brands of Christianity all claiming to have an edge on the others regarding truth.

What's truly distressing is that even *within* each of these there are many different factions claiming spiritual superiority! The "saved" think they know who is "unsaved." The "spirit-filled" have it over the noncharismatic. The orthodox look down on "liberals." It's a mess. Secondly, what others and I have been seeking has always been an answer to the question: Is there some deeper spiritual vision that can bypass all of this—interfaith and intrafaith splits alike—and hold out promise for the ultimate unity of all humanity?

Today I'm being surprised by the answer coming through.

THE SEED OF GOD
IS PLANTED IN EVERYONE

———————

Most quarterbacks about to throw a pass have the choice of a receiver made for them. There's usually only one man open. But you occasionally see so many players in the clear, the quarterback becomes almost catatonic, frozen in the face of too many options, and so is ingloriously sacked. This scenario reminds one of the mosquito that wandered into a nudist colony and collapsed under the burden of the required decision-making.

It's a bit like that trying to answer the question as to whether, when the critiquing is over, there is any truly joyous message left for Christianity to proclaim today. In truth, however, there's so much it's really hard to know where to begin. If it were otherwise, I would have found another profession quite a while ago.

No, it's not my business to convert people to Christianity. A long way back I saw the folly of believing in only one gateway or path connecting us with the mystery of God—what the famous theologian Paul Tillich referred to as the "Ground of All Being." One of the wonderful things about covering religion for the *Toronto Star* over the years was in coming to know and see God's likeness in people of every faith in the world. What's more, if I were asked today for my basic sense of identity or place in the cosmos, it would be first and foremost as a human being, a dweller on planet Earth, and not as a Christian.

But as the old country-and-western song has it, "Everybody's got to be somewhere," and that somewhere—religiously speaking—for me, is within Christianity. I was first born into it. Later, though, as an adult, I thought and committed myself to it on my own. I'm an uncomfortable Christian, perhaps, but a Christian all the same.

The core truths that are in the Bible and that speak to me as a man of the twenty-first century are not true because they are in the Bible. They are in the Bible because they are true. They reflect the deepest wisdom of the ages. Properly understood, they are the foundation of human life itself.

Yes, there is much in the Bible that is confusing, contradictory, at times even wholly immoral. Indeed, the Bible has been misinterpreted or wrongly applied to justify gross evils from war to genocide, from slavery to misogyny, from self-mutilation to racism. But most of the shadow side has flowed from human stupidity in insisting upon literalistic meanings where ninety-nine percent of the Bible is metaphor and imagery. Some of it is quite dated, of course. Yet it speaks to me more powerfully than any other voice in all of literature, in all of human culture or learning. It tells me the astonishing good news of who I really am, of where I originally came from, of where my ultimate destiny lies. And, best news of all, it does exactly the same for every single human being who ever has or who ever will become a member of the human family. This, then, of course, means you.

I could take a dozen starting points but let me be daring and plunge in at what the majority of Christians will recognize as a fundamental passage for the faith. It's read every Christmas. It comes in the opening lines of John's Gospel. It says that in the beginning was the Word (Logos) and this Word was with God and indeed was part of God. It says further that this Logos was the true light that gives light to every person coming into the world. And then it says, this Logos "was made flesh"—that is, incarnate.

It would take a thick book to explain all that was meant by the Logos in the thinking of the best minds both before and after the birth of Christianity. The Word expressed the full, creative, fiery energy of God, the drive and the rationality manifested in all of creation—and so much more.

Much earlier, the Stoics (Stoicism flourished from c.320 B.C.E.) said that each one of us carries a tiny seed of this Logos within us—the spermatikos logos, it was named. John says it was like a light that shines within every human being born. Briefly put, this Gospel declares that it is this very light, or presence, that has been "enfleshed" in *Homo sapiens*.

Tragically, to win the masses, the church chose to apply this to just one man, Jesus. My study of the texts over many years has shown me how fatal an error this has been. The heart of all religion is Incarnation—the divine within. But not just in one person above all others. In everyone.

We all come from God. We bear the seed of the divine within; we are going to God. That's good news!

DREAMS CAN HAVE
PROFOUND MEANING FOR OUR LIVES

————————

Many people say they never dream. Or they say that they're vaguely aware of having done some dreaming but they just can't remember any of it.

Whenever I interviewed the late Robertson Davies, and the discussion moved to dreams, he (who was a very proud Canadian) used to comment that the saddest thing about Canadians is that the majority of us never remember our dreams. His point was that he knew both from theory and experience that dreams have a lot to say about who we are, where we are and where we could be going. Dreams are the royal road to the unconscious, as Sigmund Freud once said. Throughout human history, and especially at crucial times, dreams have played a special part.

This is particularly true in the Bible and the sacred scriptures of many faiths. Throughout the first book of the Bible, Genesis (it means the beginning or origin), the dramatic stories about the patriarch Jacob are polarized around his crucial dream at the place he named Bethel or House of God.

He was alone, afraid, and in darkness—a mama's boy who was running from his brother Esau's fury. Jacob had tricked him out of his birthright by an outrageous scam. (Isaac, Jacob's father, was blind and Jacob tricked him into thinking he was Esau and thus stole the blessing reserved for the firstborn.) As night fell, he neared despair. There was only a stone for a pillow and the stars above as a roof. That night he dreamed a dream that was so vivid, so clearly a message that it changed his mood and, indeed, his whole future. It's remembered by every Jew, every Christian, and every Muslim since.

Jacob saw a ladder glowing beside his rocky bed and reaching up to the heavens. On it, angels were passing up and down between heaven and Earth. He woke in the early dawn and was startled as the dream and its meaning gradually filled his consciousness. He said to himself: "God is here in this place and I knew it not. . . . This is the gate of heaven." By "this place," he meant not just the physical place but also the place or point of turmoil he had reached in his inner life. Previously only aware of fear, guilt and loneliness, now he begins to realize that the Great Spirit is with him and God's messengers surround him. He discovers that what seemed like the end was in reality a gateway to a tremendously hopeful new beginning.

There are scores of such dreams in both Old and New Testaments. Christmas, for example, celebrates the key dreams that belong to the Nativity narratives in Matthew and Luke. Dreams are also featured in the change of consciousness essential for the "new beginning" of including the Gentiles (all non-Jews) in a universal mission to the world.

In chapter seven of my book *Would You Believe?* there is a more detailed account of dreams and their significance for one's spiritual life. If you want to go deeper, I recommend the works of Dr. Carl Jung. His entire approach to healing mind and spirit was based upon the psychoanalysis of his patients' dreams. See especially *Dreams, Memories and Reflections.*

By using Jacob's dream as an example, much of what is most helpful on the topic can be summed up as follows:

- Every dream that has a vivid, striking quality about it, or that is oft-repeated, with small variations, has some profound meaning for your life. Like Jacob, we need to keep paying attention. Almost magically, if you try, your ability to see the meaning will kick in, and grow.

- Notice that Jacob's experience is filled with rich symbols—an amazing ladder, angelic, spiritual beings ascend and descend on it, communicating between a lonely human and the Higher

Power. The universal language of our unconscious is always symbolic. Learn to look for the possible meaning of your dream symbols. The context, the place where you are at that time, will throw light on the inner or depth meaning and vice versa.

- Jacob never recorded his dream, but in the tradition he made sure his descendants preserved it orally by making it part of his legacy to his twelve sons. One of these, Joseph, was one of the most famous dreamers of all time. Many today, including myself, try to keep a diary of their most outstanding dreams. Other dreams are discarded. Some frivolous dreaming is simply mental knitting or the unconscious free-floating, having fun.

- You'll find that your "big" dreams most often occur at crisis times—good or bad. This is one way the Creator has planned to be with us and assist us throughout life's journey. As we look for guidance, for inspiration, for renewed hope, our inner resources are summoned to action. The Spirit stirs and announces His presence while we sleep. We often find, with Jacob, and to our great surprise and joy that God was already "in this place," but until the dream, we "knew it not."

HEAVENS STILL DECLARE
THE GLORY OF GOD

The Gnostic Gospel of Thomas holds up a wise ideal in the saying: "Become passers by." In other words, don't invest too heavily in those things that only feed the seductive illusion that this world is your permanent home. Henry Thoreau's well-remembered advice—"Simplify, simplify"—also tells us to travel light.

Our recent move to an old farmhouse in the countryside was an attempt to do that. Moving gave me and Susan, my wife, a chance to shed like an old snakeskin a lot of accumulated baggage, but unfortunately showed us that we still have way too much stuff, so that task continues.

One of the simplest delights of country living, though, has been rediscovering the night sky. One evening in September, and for the first time in a few years, we stood outside in the absolutely total dark except for the starlight. It was a sudden, transcendental, mystical experience. The silence was so profound you could feel it as a presence. The clear keening of a lonely coyote off in fields to the north only rendered it deeper still. The stars were so close, so bright, and so overpoweringly beyond belief in their infinite numbers that they took our breath away. The constellations Orion and the Big Dipper gleamed brilliantly and made us wish we knew the names of all the other configurations spread out in that enormous vault with the huge arc of the Milky Way as their setting. I realized we were looking at the most ancient Bible ever known—the heavens which "declare the glory of God," as the Psalmist says.

It's truly impossible to put into words the sense of awe, wonder, yes and worship, that enveloped us in the stillness. You felt you were standing in the presence of the holy, of that vast mystery we call

God. It was easy to understand why the theologian Rudolph Otto wrote of "the holy" as that great *mysterium tremendum et fascinosum*—the mystery that makes you both inwardly tremble and at the same time feel filled with an ineluctable yearning and attraction.

Later that same night, the full moon rose and cast its wide path—a shimmering gleam across Georgian Bay's distant waters— and the coyote howled once more. We went to bed content while the stars continued their timeless dance above.

Before going to sleep that night, I practised something I find very inspiring and helpful in trying to walk a spiritual path in today's divided world. In my imagination, I saw myself on a tiny spaceship, a kind of flying saucer. I imagined moving up through the roof of the house and up into the darkness above. Gathering speed, I could soon look down upon a vast sweep of the surrounding countryside. There were twinkling lights of other farms and over there the glow of the town. Then, in my mind's eye, I went higher and higher. Soon I could see the extended nexus of the Great Lakes below and then the whole of central Canada, and after that the entire western hemisphere was at my feet.

As I ascended into space, the whole Earth soon was spinning like a great ball that receded ever farther and farther into the limitless abyss below. Before long, there it was: that purple planet so soon to become what Carl Sagan termed "a pale blue dot."

I could see no walls down there, could hear no divisive creeds, could discern no nationalities, skin colours or political ideologies. The idea that some groups of humans there judged others to be damned or inferior because of sexuality, race, religion or political party seemed too absurd to ponder. The concept that anyone or any "ism" on that fragile piece of floating, cosmic dust could tell six billion others any exclusivist truth or command their total obedience seemed wholly ludicrous.

The idea of a "religious right" holding a monopoly of an assumed higher moral ground while blessing violence, or the concept of an American Empire which unilaterally—inspired and called by God— has a mandate to wage preemptive war in the name of peace, seemed symptomatic of insanity. I became aware as never before of the fundamental unity in which all the dwellers down there share by virtue of their common "passengership" upon that frail, round planet.

THE IMPORTANCE OF GRATEFULNESS

In Plato's *Apology*, Socrates gave us his famous dictum: the unexamined life is not worth living. Truly profound. What he didn't add, however, was the equally powerful truth that the rigorously examined life is no picnic either. It's difficult, and at times daunting. Yet it's the only road if we're serious about developing true spirituality and an increasing depth to our lives.

Genuine, daily, tough-minded yet not sadistic self-examination thrives on honesty and inevitably necessitates change. To see a blockage, a blind spot, a sin of omission or of commission—or any other shadow from past or present on the mirror of the soul—is to be challenged to act, and to be transformed.

Here's an example from my own life. I have long known, from experience as well as wide reading, that having a thankful heart and steadily giving thanks for all the blessings of this life is an essential part of living an examined life. This is true in particular on those days when we may feel the worst—preoccupied with our own needs, wants or failures. Cultivating thankfulness brings us fresh hope. What has happened can happen again despite how we feel or how strong our faith may be at any given moment.

Recently, I wrote that the British had done a better job than North Americans of preserving the wild and rural landscape of the countryside. While doing some meditative self-examination, I suddenly became aware of a large error of omission where thankfulness is concerned. I realized that I have never publicly expressed the great debt of gratitude I owe to the people of the United Kingdom in general and to the many generous couples in particular who provided incredibly warm hospitality when my friends and I were students there.

Canadians and other Commonwealth soldiers, sailors and air-men who served abroad in the Second World War will remember with gratitude an organization known as the Dominions Overseas Trust, headed by Miss Macdonald of the Isles, of Sloane Square, London. She founded the trust to gather a network of well-off English, Welsh, Scottish and Irish couples who were willing to offer their hospitality to these young men and women so far from home. They could stay for a week or more as honoured guests.

What was equally wonderful was that when the war ended, the trust directors, at Macdonald's prompting, continued offering the project's benefits to all Commonwealth students who came up to Oxford or Cambridge. In the early fifties, near the middle of my first term, all of us from Canada, New Zealand and the rest received invitations which said that if we had some free time during the up-coming eight-week Christmas vacation, we could stay free of charge in our choice of location in the rural parts of the U.K. We could go with a fellow student and climb mountains, visit cathedrals, fish for salmon or shoot grouse, depending on our allurements and the season.

This offer was also extended at Easter and again before the "long vac" of summer. As a youth from very humble origins in the east end of Toronto, who wouldn't have been at Oxford except for having won an all-expenses scholarship there for three years, I had to pinch myself once more. It was a remarkable act of kindness and welcome and I took advantage of it four times. Twice I went with a Jamaican friend, Derrick, from my college, Oriel, and twice on my own.

Each was a unique experience. The first Christmas, we spent a week in a vicarage on the wild, northeast coast of Scotland near Nairn, then for a week in the Highlands. The house was a renovated croft (shepherd's cottage) overlooking Glen Urquart, Urquart Castle, and the waters of Loch Ness. The owners, a retired English officer and his wife, told us their front yard was reputed to be one of the best sites for glimpsing the fabled monster.

Our host, who made his own potato wine, or vodka, and enthu-siastically enjoyed the fruits of his labour, said he had seen Nessie often. This was no surprise. We, however, saw no trace. But the calm beauty of the folds of hills stretching away forever and the still waters of the loch were more than enough to compensate. Our generous hosts invited us to come back shortly for Hogmanay (New Year's) and we promptly accepted. It was one of the liveliest, most welcoming New Year's experiences of my life.

My other two visits were in the south of England. One was to a mansion-like home in Dorset, near a small, ancient village. The other was the rambling rectory of an historic (Saxon) parish church deep in the Sussex Downs. The rector was an authority on insects, particularly spiders. He liked demonstrating how they spin their webs!

To all these gracious, giving people, my deepest thanks at last.

EVERY HUMAN'S A UNIQUE EPIPHANY
OF HIDDEN GOD

God must be thought of as the inconceivably transcendent:
all thoughts of that psychotic ape Homo sapiens
being divine have to be dismissed.
— Northrop Frye's Late Notebooks, 1985–1990

———————

Northrop Frye, a man of towering intellect, rightly admired and remembered for his brilliant insights into literature in general and the Bible in particular, is a hero in my private gallery. But, like all heroes, he had the right to be wrong at times and in the above quote he definitely is. Before saying why, however (because enormous issues are at stake), it is worthwhile tasting the wit of the full passage from which these few words were taken.

Frye went on to complete his thought thus:

> The sheer bumptiousness of Carl Sagan and others who want to communicate with beings in other worlds amazes me. They should be saying: look there are several billion yahoos here robbing, murdering, torturing, exploiting, abusing, and enslaving each other: they're stupid, malicious, superstitious, and obstinate. Would you like to look at the .0001 per cent of them who are roughly presentable?

This elitist and at the same time radically bleak view of his fellow human beings makes for a great quip in a university senior common-room atmosphere but is a poor plank upon which to build any theological edifice. It's close to a doctrine of total human depravity dear to some ultraconservative preachers of the past but clearly not reflective of the great man's total take on our condition. Read out of context it could be used in justification for what Charles Darwin in his autobiography justly refers to as "a damnable doctrine," that is, that of an everlasting punishment in hell for sinners. Frye certainly did not believe in that.

What though of his making God so wholly "transcendent" or "other" as to preclude the very thought of our participating in the divine nature?

It is indeed true that in his/her essential being God is utterly beyond anything we can even imagine. However, a deity who is too completely and "inconceivably" distant, alien and remote is of no relevance or use whatever to humanity. Joseph Campbell, the great master of mythology, makes this point vigorously in his PBS TV series *The Power of Myth*, with Bill Moyers. There is no way such a presence can touch our lives. The experience and teaching of all the world's greatest spiritual gurus, mystics and religious founders insist upon this salient point. The only fitting response to one who is so utterly other would be total silence.

What has endlessly fascinated me in a lifelong study of such matters is the way in which at the heart of all the world's faiths— with the possible exception of some strict forms of Buddhism— there is an insistence that although God is at one level hidden (*a deus absconditus*), nevertheless he/she is the One who, ultimately, is discovered within us all. In all religions, particularly when you look at the mystical traditions at their very centre, full humanity develops only when you become aware of who you really are and of the nearness of God as the very ground of your being.

Christianity, for example, is about Incarnation—the divine mingling with the human. Like Judaism, and Islam, it holds that *Homo sapiens* is "made in the image of God." Unfortunately, early on the mistake was made by the emerging church—attempting to bring in the greatest numbers of the unlettered throng— that God in man literally meant "God in a particular, unique individual alone" instead of God in every one of us at the core of our existence.

Plato and the other founders of Hellenic religion had taught for centuries that we are in a deep sense "fallen gods" who live in this world upon the cross of matter, learning, growing, and destined ultimately to return to full glory with God. Plato taught: "Man in body is an animal; in intellect, he is a god."

The Hebrew Psalms say quite plainly: "You are all gods and children of the most high," a statement which John's Gospel later puts in the mouth of Jesus. The Sufi (Muslim mystic) Al-Junayd (who died in 910) taught that union with God does not destroy our natural capabilities but fulfills them: The one who discovers God within will then "become more fully human." The sense of alienation from a distant God would then be over. In other words, quoting theologian Karen Armstrong, "God was not a separate, external reality and judge but somehow one with the ground of each person's being."

The truth is that the thing uniting all the world's religions at their deepest level is the belief, based upon experience, that every human being is a unique epiphany of the hidden God, expressing him/her in a particular, unrepeatable manner.

It is this profoundly transformative message that is so urgently needed at this hour of history. If every member of every faith on Earth truly was taught this and profoundly believed and lived in its light, the course of human evolution could be radically challenged and changed.

IT IS OUR DUTY
TO FIND THE DIVINE WITHIN US

As I mature, the more urgent the task becomes in my mind of us boldly taking our own evolution in hand. The idea that we must "leave it to God"—as though the Mind of the Universe regards us as children to be dragged along willy-nilly—or to mechanistic forces far beyond our control, is in reality an abrogation of both our own potential and our responsibility. It's a formula for disaster.

Some progress is being made. We are evolving steadily. The question still is: How and in what direction? For many of us, though, it's time to wake up and realize that our lives are about much more than the pursuit of happiness or simply killing time until sunset manor looms.

This is where today's religious leaders have an incredible opportunity and an inescapable duty. Their crucial task as one looks at the contemporary scene is to hammer night and day on one fundamental theme. It's not about "saving souls" or "pastoring the feeble" or even "social action," however laudable its aims may be. Their first and foremost call from God is to drum the truth into people about who they really are.

What a lot of time is wasted in Sunday sermons preaching a pedestrian kind of morality that is put across far more cogently in the average Rotary or Lions Club every week. Think of how many thousands of people go home every Sunday from church with only the most meagre pickings to chew on for spiritual fare. It's all well meaning and perhaps harmless but hardly the stuff of which a vibrant and vigorous new approach to personal, social and global problems is made.

Each of us needs to be constantly confronted with the truth that we are the very bearers of the divine presence of the Living God within our hearts and minds. We are illumined and sustained by the true light that "gives light to every human being who comes into the world." We are children of the King of Kings and yet go about half-awake as though we are the offspring of paupers.

The early religions of the Greco-Roman world all had sacred mysteries at their centre, mysteries which those who were initiated into their ranks came to prize beyond all else because they were held to lead to life abundant here and life eternal in the age to come. Well, the mystery we have been privileged to share in has been described by the Apostle Paul in these glowing terms: "And this is the Mystery, the Christ is in you, the basis of your hope of glory."

The Christ within denotes the divine presence spoken of above and it can't be stated too often that examination of every major faith in the world reveals that they bear at their centre this same teaching however differently they choose to describe or name it. The more I study other faiths the more I am impressed with the universality of this central belief in each of us possessing a touch or spark of divinity within.

Once this is grasped and fully applied to ourselves and to our relationships with all others, everything begins to change. Gone are the old labels, the old divisions based on creeds or rituals or the vagaries of religious dress. Gone too are the harsh judgments of those who worship differently, love differently or who fail to jump through the hoops of our particular belief systems.

The recognition of what it really means to be completely human, that is, to have grasped that the secret of our humanity lies in our potential for divinity, reaches beyond all that separates the various blocs and factions around the entire globe. The result is not a boring homogeneity or sameness. It means that beneath the colour and rich-ness of the full, kaleidoscopic, human tapestry of beliefs, customs and mores, there is a basic, common substratum—a metaphysical or spiritual core upon which genuine planetary unity, justice and harmony can build.

This foundation is essential for any lasting world peace. Justice flows from the recognition that every single person on the face of the Earth is made in God's image and carries the worth and dignity that attend every child of the Creator. The moral imperative—in a nuclear world—of total non-violence then remains no longer a pious ideal but the logical and necessary outcome of consciously claiming and being what we already are.

BLUEBIRDS SIGNAL SIGNS OF HOPE

I vividly remember finding and observing my first bluebird's nest in an orchard when I was about ten years old. I discovered it while investigating a cavity in the bough of a huge, aged apple tree. A sunburst of an amazing blue had just flashed from it.

It was one of those litmus experiences of youth that remain indelibly imprinted not just in the mind but in heart and soul as well. The emotions accompanying that first glimpse of a unique kind of glory made this a peak moment. Of course, I left the nest untouched.

Tragically, most people, even ardent birdwatchers, have missed out on even seeing bluebirds, never mind peeking into a nest full of eggs. For decades in the past century, bluebirds were a swiftly diminishing breed. The contamination of the planet by our unrestrained use of pesticides and herbicides, especially DDT, and first boldly documented by Rachel Carson in her bombshell book *Silent Spring*, in 1962, had come close to wiping them out altogether.

The great miracle is that they are making a wonderful comeback, slowly but surely. As a lifelong, amateur naturalist—the other kids at high school called me "nature boy" as well as "egghead"—I've kept an eye out for bluebirds over the years and have had only three or four sightings until the past couple of years.

Ever since we moved to a farm in rural Ontario in 1998, my wife and I have seen them often at a distance; scintillating flourishes of blue flitting in and about well-positioned wooden boxes erected especially for them on fence posts.

But imagine our surprise and delight this spring when we discovered them scouting out some boxes we had placed close to the house and one behind the shed. By mid-May it became clear that the bluebirds had decided to stay. So, a lifelong dream has come true. There are two families of bluebirds now living and growing near us, and sometimes, as the parents struggle to find enough grubs and other insects to feed their demanding young, it can seem like the air around is filled with them.

The truly remarkable thing is that neither of us has ever seen so many varied species of birds abounding as there are this spring and summer. Birdhouses close to our door are filled with house wrens, swallows, woodpeckers and others. Mourning doves coo from the hydro wires; the lilac and other trees hold nests of robins, hummingbirds, warblers and many more. Turkey vultures soar majestically as they circle in the updraft along the ridge that rises just behind our house or above the undulating hills across the valley.

The sound of all of them—except the vultures—singing at dawn and throughout the day, even in the rain, is bird music on a scale I had never experienced. One is reminded of Beethoven's "Ode to Joy" from the Ninth Symphony. Carson's dire predictions of a totally silent doom have been averted, at least for now.

This phenomenon is a miracle in the sense that it's something to marvel at. Yet it would never have happened if the same species that was destroying the Earth and all its inhabitants had not finally put collective effort and skill into making a new start. Millions in North America still value their lawns and gardens over birds and animals, but DDT and other lethal sprays have been banned. Birdhouses have been built to replace holes once provided by old-style fruit trees. A total program of conservation and improved habitat has been put in place.

There is a great deal to learn and to reflect upon in this simple account. It's one of the many spiritual lessons Susan and I have been gathering since the snow vanished back in April. The full picture of the environmental shambles our materialistic techno-culture has mired us in is terribly depressing to witness and to keep reading about.

But the return of the bluebirds and other once-threatened bird species such as wild turkeys, in abundance right now, incontestably demonstrates that it's not too late for a global change of consciousness, a true repentance, or as the Bible calls it in the Greek, a *metanoia:* a total change of direction. We can begin to undo the mess. There is at least a glimmer of genuine hope for a different future than the worldwide biospheric collapse predicted by many ecological experts.

We looked back out the kitchen window this morning to watch a very large jackrabbit leisurely loping across the lawn and into a cloistered stand of white pines beyond. He seemed king of the morning. He had a bird chorus that eclipsed even the great Handel to accompany him.

It seemed a sign. God seemed to be saying Eden may not be forever lost. It's possibly still within our power to regain.

THE KELSON (KEEL)
OF CREATION IS LOVE

A reader whose literary violin has but one string, and a sour one at that, sent a letter the other day arguing that my convictions about the spiritual nature of the universe are an illusion. He wrote:

> The sentiments you express have absolutely no meaning for the parents of murdered children and many other victims. Your sentiments apply to the world of your own imagination. You forget that when you die and the blood stops flowing in your brain, all the thoughts and imaginations which make you a unique individual vanish; they are erased forever.

This correspondent is but one of a stable of such stalwarts who fire off angry letters to challenge any reasoned statement in the media of belief in an Intelligence or Creator-Spirit at the core of all being. These people do not lack formidable arguments for their bleak outlook. Certainly there is an extraordinary contrast between the message of the carols and the church services at Christmas, for example, and the stories of disasters, cruelties and war always coming at us from all sides through the media. The problem of why the innocent suffer is not something to be lightly sloughed off.

Yet, with eyes wide open to all of the pain, the tears and the torment, with a profound awareness of the cries that go up from planet Earth unceasingly, it is still the deepest conviction of my heart that this cosmos of ours is founded and wrapped by love. I am persuaded that in the end all things work together for good, not just for some holy huddle of the "saved" of this or that religious persuasion, but for every creature. What's more, together with many millions down the ages, I believe in a destiny for every creature in which "all things will be made new."

Coincidentally, the same day the letter above arrived, I was browsing through Walt Whitman's famous *Leaves of Grass* and came upon those lovely lines:

> *And I know that the hand of God is the elderhand of my own,*
> *And I know that the spirit of God is the eldest brother of my own,*
> *And that all the men ever born are also my brothers . . . and the*
> *women my sisters and lovers,*
> *And that a kelson of the creation is love. . . .*

Like you (most probably), I hadn't the slightest notion what the word "kelson" meant, and so I reached for a dictionary. The *Penguin Canadian Dictionary* didn't have it listed. I had better luck with the *Concise Oxford Dictionary*. It said the word derives from "keel"— as of a boat—and an unexplained suffix, "son." The reference is to the line of timber used to fasten the floor timbers at the bottom of a ship to its keel. In Whitman's imagery, the meaning is then clear. He is saying that the very foundation of the universe is love. Experts on Whitman and his poetry know that this is indeed a grounding theme of his work and that his vision of life itself stemmed from an ongoing, mystical insight into the nature of things, a kind of Cosmic Consciousness.

Whitman, who belonged to no church and scandalized many faithful by his enthusiastic affirmation of the body and the senses, did not believe in the ultimate goodness of God and in life after death because of some Pollyanna-ish, wishful thinking. What strikes you as you read him and struggle with the various levels of meaning is that here is a man who knew life intimately in all its rawness. For many months during the American Civil War, he worked with the wounded and the dying. He saw the torn, lacerated bodies and the agonies of minds and emotions stretched beyond all endurance. He knew that life can be hell and that hate and injustice often seem to be in control. Yet, he "knew" that the kelson of creation is divine love.

As I reflected on Whitman, it came to me with renewed force that this same vision is the one motivating all the great "saints" of humanity, from Socrates to Gandhi and Mother Teresa. Indeed, in my years of travelling the remoter parts of the globe in search of stories for the *Toronto Star,* one thing always stood out above all others. The people who were truly doing something about suffering and pain were almost universally those who believed, as Whitman did, that behind all appearances to the contrary love is the fire and energy of life. None of them lived in an ivory tower. Quite the contrary, they were in the eye of the storm.

Where others curse the darkness and give in to apathy and despair, heroes like Jean Vanier at l'Arche, Mother Teresa and the Reverend Mark Buntain in Calcutta, and Dr. Helen Huston in the hinterland of Nepal look these evils in the eye and triumph over them because they "know" the final victory is already assured and won.

PRAYER SENDS GOD
OUT INTO DISTANT SKIES

―――――――――

"Our Father which art in heaven. . . ." These words, which begin what is the most widely recited, best-known prayer in the world, remind one at times of reflection of a street signpost that has been mischievously turned the wrong way around. They are only six words, but taken at their literal, surface value they have actually done real harm and caused spiritual loss to many. For these, they have pointed the wrong way.

Let's begin by looking at the first two words, "Our Father." As stressed in my book *Prayer: The Hidden Fire*, many people whose experience of their own father was damaging in one way or another are not much helped by the metaphor of fatherhood. Suppose they were sexually abused by their father; suppose they have always felt a deep sense of abandonment because of a completely absent father or a father who was cold and aloof—or domineering, violent or verbally abusive.

We must face it. Mothers are the "makers of spirit," as one of John Wesley's biographers remarked, but it is largely through memories of one's father that initial conceptions of God are formed. However, the total maleness of the "Our Father" imagery has unconsciously shaped the entire church's approach to the feminine principle of life in general and women in particular. Patriarchy hinges entirely on a male-only understanding of the divine and his/her relationship with each of us.

Feminist theologians have done us all a great service in drawing attention to this vast flaw in Christian thinking, that is, that God is wholly male. The Ultimate Source of all things is neither male nor female but utterly beyond gender. Those who find the words "Our Father" deleterious in their overall approach to God should drop them at once and substitute whatever works more appropriately for them. Just say "Our God" or "Our Father-Mother" or something else. God knows our hearts before and while we pray. Unlike us, God is not hung up on theological correctness. As Paul says, even our groanings and incoherencies of the heart are known to the Spirit as the deepest prayers of all.

It is the next four words—"which art in heaven"—that cause the greatest concern. Because of them, western Christianity has for twenty centuries projected the Author of All Being out into distant skies—somewhere far off, anywhere but here. This has had huge consequences for religious understanding and for evolving human behaviour. God has essentially been a "sky-god" or one who sits above the clouds—as in the Sistine Chapel, pictured above—intervening whimsically now and then. But the original version and words were, thankfully, not talking spatially or literally. The phrase "in heaven" is not even found in the earliest manuscripts of Luke's version (11:2). The official Bible Societies' Greek text just begins, "Father, let your name be kept holy . . ." It's there in Matthew (6:9ff): "Our Father who art in heaven . . ." but the words signify a state rather than a place of being. In other words, no matter how far into the skies a spaceship might travel in years to come it will never arrive at a region or galaxy called or constituting heaven.

The expression, then, refers to a reality quite unlike anything else we can comprehend or know with our senses. It's an attempt to express the otherness of God, or, if you like, the truth that there is an entirely numinous, beyond-the-imagination Source of All Being which is all-powerful and all-knowing yet infinitely and ultimately caring in spite of any appearances to the contrary. The heart of all reality is love. To use an analogy, though a not entirely satisfactory one, the reality of heaven in relation to the material world is like that of the parallel universes or interlocking universes now being discussed by leading scientists. (To his credit, philosopher

and author Deepak Chopra has done much to illumine the mysteries of this invisible reality of Spirit through his grasp of quantum physics.)

The problems the church faces in meeting the questions and
needs of the world today are the result largely of failing to realize
that a "God out there" no longer speaks to us. Neglect of such Gospel
teachings as "The Kingdom of God is within you" or Paul's oft-
repeated phrases "in Christ" or "Christ in you," has abetted the
impression of God's remoteness off in the starry realms. So, too, has
ignoring the pagan-sourced quotes in Acts that we are "God's offspring" and that "In him we live and move and have our being."

YOUR HORIZONS ONLY CHANGE
WHEN YOU MOVE

————————

When I was a boy growing up on Lawlor Avenue in Toronto's east end, I often hiked the long distance to the top of the Scarborough Bluffs. I'd go after school or on weekends, sometimes with another kid, more often on my own. I used to go in all seasons and would spend time just looking out at the lake. Occasionally, on an exceptionally clear day, I could see the other side and a faint cloud of mist indicating Niagara Falls. The sense of freedom and of dreams as yet unrealized that welled up in me at such times was a tremendous source of empowerment—though I wouldn't have known how to express that then. Anything seemed possible.

Since I kept up this almost Buddhist-like form of meditation right through high school, until I went to university and moved into residence on the University of Toronto campus in the heart of the city, it played an essential part in my "formation," to use a churchy term.

Analyzing it all these years later, I have realized that for me, as for many of you, spending time just looking off into the distance and meditating or mindfully studying the horizon has been a central feature of my whole life right up to the present. It's one reason my wife and I have chosen to live in a rural area. Nearly every day, out walking with my dog, Buddy, winter or summer I get at least a brief few moments to look off into the distance at what I call the "notch," a part of the Niagara Escarpment that looks like a vast river mouth, with steep high cliffs on either side and the bright gleam of Georgian Bay in the background. Bald eagles nest there in season.

This natural setting helps keep things in perspective. For example, I know that those cliffs were limestone seabeds once, formed countless millions of years ago and then thrust up into the air by some cataclysmic shifting of the Earth's surface. They stretch all the way up to Tobermory at the tip of the Bruce Peninsula. Given that scale and time span, any other issue, however troubling, gets scaled down significantly. Nature can do that for most of us when given the chance. Just one look at the night sky in the country will confirm that.

The whole concept of a horizon leads to deeper things. Seeking to define its literal meaning would lead us to something like: "The horizon is where land or water or the city's sprawl meets the sky." Putting it somewhat more philosophically, we could say: "The horizon is our limit of vision. It's as far as we can see." The next stage is then an easy one. We move to metaphor, and the horizon becomes for us our limit of vision or of "seeing" mentally or spiritually. In this sense, we all have very specific "horizons"—and they, too, were formed long ago. Many of them came into place in our earliest years.

For some, these "limits of vision" have become very rocklike indeed. As a matter of fact, without our knowing it at times, they have become like circling cliffs that hem us in and limit or cut off glimpses of other vistas, other insights, other possibilities. In a letter this week, a young reader with two university degrees described how recently he has been breaking free of the "invisible shackles of constraining beliefs" and gaining a new spiritual understanding. His horizons are changing. Understandably, the sight of the fear their traditional faith has instilled in his parents' eyes—"They are terrified of death and the consequences that face them from a God of their old notions," he said—moves him with deep compassion.

Sadly, millions are still trapped by outworn guilt and fear-based religious teachings that loudly pretend to enhance human happiness but, in reality, cramp and confine the essence of joy itself. Sacred institutions initially set up to further human liberation have too often used their power to control their flocks and to inhibit genuine spiritual maturity. As the Gospels strikingly say, their leaders and advocates neither enter the Kingdom of Heaven themselves nor do they permit others to do so. Hard words, but true.

The real question here is: How do you set about getting a fresh vision, a new and wider horizon for mind and spirit? The one thing I know from personal experience with horizons is that they only truly change when you move from where you are. Of course, I intend this metaphorically. You must find a new "place" to stand, preferably a piece of "higher ground." Nobody can hand this to us. Beware of those who would coerce. But find it we must, personally, as a society, yes, and as a species too.

NURTURE SEED OF DIVINE SPIRIT

Recently I had written that the Bible, which is a collection of books rather than one book, keeps asking us deep, inescapable questions. These questions are not in any way aimed solely at people with a "religious bent." They are existential, that is, life-bearing, searching, tuned-into-reality probings that are designed to push forward the immense task of human evolution.

We are not here simply to replicate ourselves through propagation and to greedily devour the fruits of the Earth as we constantly quest for gain, fame and pleasure. Each human life is meant to move the species ahead, be it ever so slightly, towards the full coming of the divine order—known metaphorically as the Kingdom of God. Then will be fulfilled the ancient prayer: "Your Kingdom come, your will be done on Earth as it is in Heaven." We have very far to go. Our track record at times is depressingly poor. In truth, even the institutions organized to forward this evolutionary thrust seem to forget about it altogether. Often they set it back badly. They get mired in self-preoccupation or the "edifice complex," or the lust for control.

To assist us in our vast undertaking, there is a single, overwhelming question that is hurled at us from the pages of the sixty-six books of the Bible—indeed, from all the sacred scriptures of the world, Sikh, Hindu, Buddhist, Muslim and those of other religions. Upon its answer everything depends.

The question thundering forth is: Who are you? In other words, who or what is a human being? Yes, this query is often coded or hidden by archaic, symbolic imagery. Most of the scriptures of the world's great religions flow out of cultures and ways of speaking of the eternal that differ vastly from our own. Consequently, the true inner meaning is often missed or distorted beyond recognition by our plodding, surface-focused outlook on life.

One of the greatest challenges for genuine spiritual leaders today is to assist contemporary humans to pierce through the hoary literalisms to the jewels hidden in the wrappings of religion. But at times you'd hardly know its urgency. For example, listening to many sermons today or reading books aimed at restoring Christianity to some semblance of relevance for the twenty-first century, one often listens in vain to hear anything of this question or, even more important, of the answer to it.

Who or what are you? How you and I give or understand the answer to this one ultimatum determines the entire fabric, meaning and direction of our lives. It shapes the way we treat ourselves and others. It undergirds our sense of purpose and meaning. It directs how we use or allow our bodies to be used. Hence it has enormous relevance for the issue of human sexuality—for what popular parlance so superficially refers to as one's "sex life." (As though sexuality can be divorced from the complete texture of the warp and woof of our body-mind-soul reality!)

There is but one answer to the issue of who and what we are and, like the question itself, it too flows from nearly every page of Holy Writ for those who see or are helped to see it for themselves. It has nothing to do with belonging to a particular faith. No leader has a monopoly or alone holds the keys to this treasure lode.

After much study devoted to such matters, I am totally convinced that those are right—those very few—who contend that the one datum or fundamental fact at the heart of all religion is that of Incarnation. By that I mean that each of us is not simply a son or daughter of God but that by natural birthright we have a latent divinity within. This truly can be expressed in a hundred ways. We "live and move and have our being" in God, as a pagan poet quoted by St. Paul in his famous sermon in Athens once described it. Or, we have the "seed" of the divine Logos (as in the Parable of the Sower in the Gospels or in Stoic thought) within us.

Every faith has its own way of describing this inner spark, flame, essence, "image of God" or inner Christ. Paul said the entire "mystery" at the heart of Christianity lies in this one truth: "Christ (or the Christ) within you!" But if that is who we really are, the carriers of the sacred, divine Spirit, then our highest responsibility and task is to nurture this seed, to fan this flame, to bring this infant Christ to full maturity in our lives. Only that can change the world.

ON MAKING A DIFFERENCE

The renowned American poet Robert Frost once wrote about his epitaph:

> *I would have written of me on my stone:*
> *I had a lover's quarrel with the world.*

Have you ever given thought to how you would want your own epitaph to read? It's a challenging, and sometimes life-transforming, exercise. Earlier on, I used to think about "To Be Continued" as a possibility—an affirmation of faith and hope in the life of "the age to come." But, of late, I've changed. Right now, I don't think there can be a more meaningful phrase to sum up someone's existence than "He (or she) made a difference." This epitaph focuses on positive action in the here and now; on the well-being of others; it's a call of hope because it affirms that things can be changed; and it summons everyone both individually and collectively to do and to be better than we are.

It's often a temptation just to sit back and do nothing as the endless media litany of the threats, dangers, miseries, injustices, famines and wars that modern life provides almost overwhelms our senses. What's the use of resisting? many ask. But as a study of history reveals, our species contains within it a special grace of the divine whereby "all things are possible." There has always been a determined minority who, with that vision and power, have made the difference.

I've thought a great deal about what it takes to help make a difference:

- One key thing is an act of will. It means resolving to be part of the answer rather than part of the problem. The old adage about lighting a candle rather than cursing the darkness is profoundly true. Will it, and believe it. You'll see for yourself.

- Don't expect a mass movement. As Henry Thoreau once said, "When have the good and the brave ever been a majority?" There's a reason the Jesus of the Gospels spoke about his followers being like yeast in a lump of dough or like truly salty salt. Small actions by a few can have huge results. It's the dedicated few who have caught a vision of what can be, who bring the change that makes the difference.

  Nobody in the first century C.E. would have predicted that the tiny, mocked group of people called Christians would eventually be victor over the vast power and glory of imperial Rome. Nobody six hundred or so years later would have predicted that Muhammad would eventually be followed as the Prophet of Allah by over a billion people.

- You need more, however, than willpower, vision and dedication. Everyone who wants to help meet either world issues or the needs of those closest to them must have some inner source of power or special energy. Today, the most potent recovery/healing groups, for example, all share a common element: they stress the need for becoming aware of the spiritual resources within and around us. It's drawing on the strength of a Higher Power that brings the courage, hope, wisdom and vision to keep on going on.

- Making a difference requires a strategy suited to the problem. The core is exactly what Mother Teresa said to me years ago in an interview in Calcutta about her approach to the seemingly impossible: "You must first see and analyze the need; then, do all in your power to meet it. One step, one person, at a time." The principle is clear, its application is infinitely variable.

- One must face the costs involved, especially the emotional and intellectual cost of full preparation for meeting the need that most fires your imagination. Costly courage and determination will be necessities in overcoming the inertia or active opposition of those whose self-interest makes them hostile to all who fight for justice and peace. Everyone, young or mature, who longs and works for a healthy environment, a nuclear-free world order and a just society will inevitably confront the powers that be. Making a difference is one of the very few heroic adventures left for us today, particularly for our young people. But it's not a free ride.

- Who are the ones being called to make a difference at this moment? Well, you and you—and I. But to return to youth for a moment. They are the ones who need most to feel the summons to see things differently and to live their lives in step with a different drummer than their peers and popular values, with all their seductions, provide.

I don't idealize or romanticize the past. But I have a deep sense that fifty years ago and beyond, young people felt a much keener sense of responsibility and were being challenged much more often to think beyond their own interests, pleasures and security than they are at present. They were encouraged to believe deeply that crucial social crises and global evils could be tackled and transformed.

Not all of them, but yet many more than we think, are waiting to become the creative minorities who can and will make a difference. We should ask and encourage them to risk doing so.

WE SHOULD NEVER
COME DOWN FROM THE WALL

––––––––––––––––

This discussion is about one of the most important ethical insights I know, but I want to begin with some thoughts about walls. I was born in the east end of Toronto yet I look on England as a second home both spiritually and in other ways. No spot on Earth has more variety and wealth of natural beauty in so small a space surrounded by such densities of population. The wild places of England especially, the moors, the fells and the mountains, touch deep regions of the heart and mind of the beholder.

At the risk of being thought eccentric, I have to confess to an obsession with English walls, not those of gardens and estates but those of the remoter countryside of Cornwall, Devon, Somerset, Yorkshire and Cumbria. Looking out from a train one can tell almost exactly where one is from the shape and texture of the walls alone, from the moss-covered boulders of Exmoor to the creamy texture of Cotswold stones or the delicately layered dry-stone walls of the Lake District. The latter bear mute testimony to centuries of hand labour as they checker the landscape and run straight up the mountainsides. With the sheep, the mists and the white cataracts—called by the Irish "the tears of the mountains"—even the memory still casts its spell.

Tempted though I am to linger there, however, I want to take you to a different clime and time and to a story about walls that is never far from my mind when I think about the way we ought to live and about a four-letter word that used to be the heart and soul of ethics—the word "duty." Today it has to be the least-used four-letter word in our vocabulary.

The story concerns the great stone walls of the ancient City of Jerusalem and is one of the many stirring narratives that once made up the normal heritage of western men and women but today have been banished to near oblivion by the tide of general ignorance of the Bible and the morass of so-called pop culture that has usurped and blotted out the past. The entire account is found in the Book of Nehemiah, and tells how the Persian king Artaxerxes grants permission to the Jew Nehemiah to go back to his native land and rebuild the walls smashed to ruins during the Persian conquest. The year was about 445 B.C.E. and the Temple, which had already been rebuilt, was sitting wholly unprotected. Without walls, the few remaining Jews in the city were defenceless as well.

Naturally, as always happens when any duty, task, project or course of action with high aims is initiated, as soon as it became clear to the world what Nehemiah was about to do, the opposition began. By the way, it is so inevitable, so completely predictable that you could call it a law. If you are determined and trying to do the right thing, no matter how small or relatively insignificant the task may be, there will always be pain, difficulty or opposition. There is a kind of moral entropy at work in the universe and it resists moral and spiritual progress. You don't have to go all mystical and bring in props like the devil to believe that this is so. You learn it in the crucible of experience. It can act through people. It can be felt in circumstances or events. There is no victory or achievement without first the dust and sweat of the struggle.

In Nehemiah's case, there was the sheer difficulty of the engineering feat involved, problems of adequate manpower and materials, and the weather. But his chief opposition, as is so often the case, came in the form of other human beings with their own ideas about how things should be done. There were enemies on every hand motivated by fear, envy and plain obstructionism. They had a vested interest in Jerusalem's vulnerability. So they feigned attacks, they made false accusations—including the charge that Nehemiah was really plotting to be king and to rebel against Artaxerxes, the distant overlord, and rule himself. They tried every other trick in the book. A particular enemy was an unsavoury character by the ugly name of Sanballat.

Nehemiah struggled to complete the walls, each man working with one hand while holding his weapon in the other. Half stood ready with their spears and took a rest as the other half laboured. Finally, having tried every other angle, Sanballat and his cohorts sent a message inviting Nehemiah to attend a "friendly" meeting to discuss the matter. Rightly suspecting that the Samaritan planned an ambush for him, Nehemiah sent the messengers back with a declaration that ranks with some of the noblest manifestos of courage in all literature. He said: "I am doing a great (important) work so that I cannot come down; why should the work cease while I leave it and come down to you?"

They sent the messengers back to plead with him five times and each time he confronted them with the same rebuke. And the walls were finally finished.

It's extremely helpful to hold a story like that deeply in your consciousness in the midst of the kind of world we live in today. It's true for the student who feels like quitting school or for the adolescent who wants to keep clean from drugs; it's true for the caregiver or public servant who is simply worn out or burned out. When the overwhelming glut of information threatens to pull us off our centre and cause us to lose our focus, when the temptation to ease or pleasure drowns out the inner clarion call to duty, when seductive voices tell us our effort won't be missed, or fears of what others may think assail, we need to hear the affirmation: "This is a great work I am doing; I cannot come down."

2

NEW HORIZONS
FOR THE JOURNEY

But when I become an adult I put away childish things.
— ST. PAUL

A RELIGIOUS SYMBOL
WITH MANY MEANINGS

The cross—"the old, rugged cross," as the familiar hymn puts it—will forever be associated with the shame, suffering, sacrifice and ultimate victory of Jesus Christ on the first God's Friday (Good Friday). But as the most primordial of all religious symbols, the cross had quite a range of wholly different meanings for untold millennia before the dawn of Christianity.

Egyptologists, for example, report that the sign of a cross was common on the breasts of mummies and that the cross was frequently placed in the hands of the dead as "an emblem both of Incarnation and of new life to come." It was carved on the back of the scarab (a gem or brooch carved into the shape of the dung beetle, another symbol) with the same meaning.

The ankh, a cross with a circle at the top, was widely used in ancient Egypt as a sign of eternal life. Crosses of all types, from swastikas to Plato's mythical divine man "stamped upon the universe," are

evident wherever so-called primitive religion is studied. For example, anthropologists have discovered equal-arm crosses carved into
rock and other hard surfaces, which date to the neolithic period.

Conservative scholars, anxious to avoid any seeming depend-
ency of Christianity upon paganism, usually take the tack of attempting to explain away the "extraordinary dissemination of the cross
through the world prior to Christianity" by calling it a "primordial
symbol related more to other symbols such as the centre, the circle,
and the square." Its most obvious use in this respect would be to
divide a circle into four even parts.

Yet, other scholars, notably the late-American linguistics and
Biblical expert Alfred Boyd Kuhn, author of *The Lost Light* and numerous other seminal books on ancient religion, has produced a
mass of evidence for a radically different point of view. A Ph.D.
from Columbia University, Kuhn was skilled in several modern and
ancient languages, including Hebrew and Egyptian hieroglyphics.

Kuhn, who is not alone in his stand, contended that the single
most important religious event to have happened in all human
history was the awakening of self-reflective consciousness. At that
precise moment, we stopped being purely animals and became
quickened as true human beings, with intellects and souls. A solely
religious version of this same phenomenon can, of course, be found
in Genesis, chapters 1 and 2. Kuhn traced the birth of all religious
impulses to this momentous creation event—the awareness that the
"horizontal" of our animality had been intersected by the "vertical"
of self-reflective reason and a profound sense of the divine.

The cross, then, in all its shapes and forms, depicted allegorically this primal experience and reality. Hence its universality. It was
a constant symbol of our rootedness in the earth on the one hand
and our destiny with God on the other. Later mystics found it to
be the ideal "plus sign" because it opened the whole way to human
development and unfolding.

Placed on its side, as the multiplication sign, the cross again
mystically represents the motion and impulse given to all life by the
intersection of spirit (the vertical) with matter. Kuhn says that in

paganism and early Christianity, "The cross is always a symbol of life, never of death, except as 'death' means Incarnation. It was the cross of life on earth because its four arms represent the fourfold foundation of the world, the four elements, earth, water, air and fire, of the human temple (or being) . . ."

That takes nothing whatever away from the rich and central importance of the cross for Christians at Easter and throughout the church year. Indeed, if anything, it adds a great deal.

Significantly, the true sign of Christianity for the earliest centuries of church history was not a crucifix but either a bare cross or one with a lamb fastened to it. According to Kuhn, in the entire iconography of the catacombs "no figure of a man on a cross appears during the first six or seven centuries of the era." Not until 692, in the reign of Justinian II, was it decreed by the church (the Trullan Council) that in future the figure of the historical Jesus should supersede "instead of the lamb, as in former times."

Psychoanalyst Carl Jung believed that one of the most important tasks of the church is to make the old symbols come alive again with renewed power. Seeing the bare cross in its true and fullest dimensions is a vital part of that.

MISREADING OF JOHN'S GOSPEL
JUSTIFIES INTOLERANCE

One of the hoariest objections raised every time one questions the exclusivist claims of conservative "Churchianity"—what I have called the "Jesus only" formula—is a verse from John's Gospel, chapter 14. Jesus allegedly says: "I am the way, and the truth, and the life. No one comes to the Father except through me."

Vaulting from these only-too-familiar words in this one, isolated text, the leap is made to the narrow conclusion that all other "ways" to the "Father" or to Transcendency, God, divine Mind, however one tries to describe the Ultimate, are at best inadequate, and at worst completely bogus.

It can't be repeated too often: This simplistic reasoning has justified much intolerance and outright violence in the church's past. It continues, especially in North America, to hinder the attempt to build a godly, compassionate and tolerant community in today's increasingly pluralistic world. Accordingly, would-be Christians have at this moment an urgent need to come to terms with what the bald, tedious repetition of this particular mantra means and to examine its assumed validity afresh.

In the first place, its source, John's Gospel, is very different from the first three (synoptic) Gospels. Any good commentary will point this out in detail. But an intelligent person who reads, say, the earliest Gospel, Mark, and then reads John, can see this truth at once. As I've said before, John's Jesus walks "about two metres above the ground." He talks in a different style; he does different things, such as the seemingly spectacular raising of Lazarus, a miracle surprisingly not even noticed by Matthew, Mark or Luke; the chronology is different; key events, such as the Last Supper, are left out. Small wonder some scholars in the early church called John the mystical or spiritual Gospel, while others wondered whether or not it should even be included in the final canon of authoritative scripture.

Clearly, whatever we have in the first three Gospels, this Jesus of John is certainly not a Jesus of history, but the Christ of the eternal Christos myth. Repeatedly in John, Jesus' sublime and lofty words echo those of earlier Christs of the Egyptian and other mythologies. Numerous similarities between this and other ancient sayings could be cited if space permitted. (I refer readers to my book *The Pagan Christ* for examples.)

The nub of the matter is this: It's my conviction, shared by many contemporary scholars, that no historical Jesus ever spoke these words which have become so important to the opponents of a truly ecumenical, truly interfaith global community. To wield them as a club is not just uncharitable; it's wrong.

However, if one is committed to a position where querying the authenticity of any Bible verse—even the most immoral or incomprehensible—is out of the question because of a prior commitment to the unprovable axiom that if it's "in the book" it's God's own word, there are still several hurdles to face.

When a holy person says that he is the "way," he is using a metaphor. Nobody is a road (Greek, *hodos*) or a "way" in any literal sense. Metaphors must always be translated or interpreted. They call for subjective judgment. The literal meaning is never the right one. As the famous American mythologist Joseph Campbell was fond of saying, it's not the denotation but the connotation that counts when you encounter a metaphor.

Furthermore, what does it mean to say that anyone, however exalted, is the "truth"? If it is going to be insisted upon that this verse be taken literally, at face value, one is surely entitled to ask: "The truth about what?" It goes without saying that Jesus was not and is not the "truth" about mathematics, about astronomy, about computer technology, behavioural medicine or a whole range of other things. (I make this obvious point simply to show that even for literalists some interpretation—and caution—is necessary in treating any Bible text.) What is being said, in the context of the chapter, refers to the way to, the truth about, and the life to be lived by, or given to, anyone seeking to know God.

What Jesus is being made to say metaphorically is that anyone seeking God must in the end come by the way which Jesus himself found, must discover the truth which he discovered leads to knowledge, and must experience the quality and character of life which he had revealed to him as the essence of being human. Like Jesus, each of us has to discover our own divine inheritance. This understanding, described in my book *The Pagan Christ,* precludes no other religion. It excludes no one.

Short of saying that the John passage is an invention, or a plagiarism from a more universal, ancient mythos, it's the only view that a person such as myself could honestly hold and still be content to call myself a Christian.

THE STORY OF JESUS
SHOWS HIS REFLECTED DIVINITY

———————

One of the most ancient religious ideas known to our race is that we are, as Plato insisted, a mixture, even a sacred "marriage," of the animal and the divine—part animal, part god. One way the ancient sages put it was: "The gods distribute divinity" to humankind. They spoke of the body as the "tomb of the soul" during our life on the earth plane. In the Greek, there was a play on the words *soma sema*, body = tomb. You get a similar concept in the Bible where Paul says that our bodies are the "temple" of God's Spirit; or again, "We have this treasure (the soul) in earthen vessels."

In true Greek philosophy and religion, however, the body was in no way evil, nor was matter itself. That was a later distortion unfortunately taken up by the church and never to this day quite overcome. For the Egyptian, the Sumerian, the Vedic and most other ancient theologies, the human was a "miracle" blending of spirit, with matter its mother. The Latin word for "mother," *mater*, is the source of our word "matter."

Since following this ancient wisdom we are all of us sharers in divinity—possessing a spark or flame of the divine within—I have argued in *The Pagan Christ* that the divinity portrayed by Jesus— whom the Bible insists was also fully human—was essentially the same as ours. He expressed or reflected it more fully in his dramatic role than the rest of us. It is a difference of degree not of kind.

This idea, though unintentionally, upsets many church people. They believe Jesus was a historical person and quite unique. They forget that if he was utterly unique (in the proper sense of that word) as an historical person, then he would be of no use to the rest of us at all! Like the saviour figure Osiris/Horus of the Egyptian myth, he was described as fully one with us.

Here, however, I'd like to clarify one issue. Nobody, no single human being—and certainly the Jesus of the Gospels never did— can ever lay any absolute claim to be God. As the German mystic Meister Eckhart once said, God is more than beingness, S/He is beyond pure being itself. Jesus said: "God is Spirit." Indeed, if ever the full measure of pure divinity were to enter a person, that individual would be instantly consumed and utterly destroyed. The Bible duly warns: "Our God is a consuming fire."

As the comparative-religions scholar Alvin Boyd Kuhn said, our possessing a portion or "unit" of the divine fire within is analogous to the way in which there is solar fire in every cell of our physical bodies. The sun's presence is active in every molecule of our being. But we are certainly not the sun nor can we stand even to gaze fully at it in all its might, let alone vainly imagine our somehow being it in its plenitude.

The spark or candle of divinity within our souls—once discovered and given air to breathe—flickers faintly through the marred and opaque "window" of our personalities and lives. Yet, as Jesus is reported saying, we are indeed the "light" to the rest of the world, that is, to all sentient and even non-sentient fellow-sharers in the biosphere. He warned, if that light within us becomes darkness "how great is that darkness!"

The goal of life is to allow and encourage this light to integrate and harmonize our animal selves into what it means to be fully human; to nurture and fuel this godly illumination so that it may shine forth ever more clearly for ourselves and others. To do that is to become "Christ conscious" or, in non-Christian terms, to give full expression to the Higher Self, the god within.

It is important to remember that all the great religions of the world have their way of expressing this core truth. As most comparative-religions scholars have discovered, all the great religious myths have as their origin this one central "true myth" of humanity—the "old, old story" of how the divine, at great cost (that's the meaning of all those crucified saviours), has shared its nature with humans forever.

We are here to gain experience, to learn, to grow. But as the great psychoanalyst Carl Jung said, echoing Paul, we have no idea of the glory that awaits the final consummation of our evolutionary journey. I call this a "Gospel" or good news, and it's for everyone.

GOSPELS WRITTEN AS
BENIGN FORM OF PROPAGANDA

———————

The question of the non-historical nature of the narratives of the Old Testament has enormous consequences for understanding the Bible and for issues as current as the present crisis in the Middle East.

For example, ultraorthodox Jewish claims to the Holy Land based upon promises to Abraham and an alleged conquest some three thousand years ago have to be viewed in a wholly new light. Christian literalists, in their turn, have to make a total about-face on their stand that every word in the Bible comes directly from the mouth of God. It's increasingly clear that the human beings composing the Old Testament played a dominant role in all that was recorded. (I refer readers to *The Bible Unearthed: Archeology's New Vision of Ancient Israel and the Origin of Its Sacred Texts*, by Israel Finkelstein and Neil Silberman.)

What about the New Testament? Surely here, if anywhere, in Holy Writ we are on historical terra firma. But once you realize that ancient authors, writing about God and God's ways with individuals and nations, always use metaphor, myth, poetry, allegory, parable and a host of other symbolic modes of writing to describe eternal truths, you have to ask why they would suddenly stop at the beginning of the Christian era. The truth is that they didn't.

The Gospels, in particular, may, like much of the Hebrew Bible, sound a little like history and even make use of historical names and places, but they are very far from what we moderns understand by that concept.

We need to read and understand these documents in the manner they were originally intended to be taken. The Gospels were originally written as a benign form of propaganda. They were not meant to impart history but to buttress and convey belief. They dealt with the inner meaning of history, not the narration of actual events.

Here's the editor of John's Gospel (the least historical of them all) stating his aims: "But these things are written so that you may come to believe that Jesus is the Messiah . . ." Luke's Gospel opens with a statement that he is adding his account to those already written by "many" others in order to set forth the "truth" about the Jesus story. This carries an impression of concern for history. But all the early chapters of this work are filled with non-historical, highly symbolic narratives.

For example, Mary's bursting into the soaring verses of the "Magnificat" upon hearing that her aged relative, Elizabeth, is also "with child," is given as a spontaneous moment. But scholars—indeed, anyone of good sense—can tell that this psalm is a well-crafted, well-studied piece of writing that nobody, let alone an untutored girl from the sticks, could suddenly improvise. It clearly depends upon Old Testament precedents.

Next, Luke tells how a decree went out from Augustus that "all the world should be registered." There is no trace—in a well-documented period—of such a decree. It's simply a means of getting Joseph and Mary to Bethlehem for theological reasons. The messiah had to be of Davidic descent and thus from Bethlehem.

The stories of the angels, the shepherds, in Luke, and of the wise men in Matthew all are rewrites of Egyptian mythical themes from over two thousand years earlier. There is no historical record whatever of Herod's alleged edict regarding the "slaughter of the innocents." Common sense alone tells us that such an order was impossible in any case. Did Herod intend to kill the children of his friends, of his soldiers, the civil service, the tourists passing through and so on and on?

You know the whole matter is symbolic for certain once you realize that this attempt to slaughter the holy child is a constant theme of all ancient hero myths, from Moses to Horus to Sargon to Hercules. Take the matter of the two genealogies of Jesus in Matthew and Luke. Clearly they have nothing to do with history and everything to do with myth.

For example, read each one and ask yourself who was Jesus' grandfather. Luke traces the family "history" to Adam because his is a universal theme. Matthew traces it from Abraham (who was not an historical figure) because he's interested in the Jewish descent. But both accounts give the entire show away when they come down to the conclusion. Both show clearly that on the father's side, Jesus was (as was compulsory) a descendant of David. But they fail to admit how utterly irrelevant this really is since, in their view, Joseph wasn't the father at all!

This, of course, is just a bare peek at the issues involved. One could go on. Virgins don't have babies. Stars don't "stand" over houses or stables. They don't lead one west, especially when they appear in the east. But they do occur in every ancient myth. That's the point. When we come, say, to the Sermon on the Mount and realize that it was never preached as a sermon at one go and that more than ninety-nine percent of it can be matched in Jewish and other writings of that period, we really begin to realize that the old literal approach is dead in the water. Yet, in this process, something quite new and liberating is about to emerge.

RESURRECTED BODY A
SPIRITUAL, NOT PHYSICAL, REALITY

I believe in . . . the Resurrection of the body . . .
— THE APOSTLES' CREED, c.390 C.E., author(s) unknown

Most thinking Christians are well aware that saying the traditional creeds is problematic, unless one interprets them as a form of symbolism or allegory. A literal interpretation makes little sense—to me or to thousands of others. Oddly, however, the one statement in the Apostles' Creed that, during university, I could not with integrity "confess" at all, symbolically or otherwise—"I believe in . . . the Resurrection of the body . . ."—now rings much clearer.

Since confusion is so rampant among believers and non-believers alike as to what is meant by "the Resurrection of the body," I'm going to try to set out the issues as I see them now. Obviously not even the Pope can claim absolute certainty in such matters.

We know that the doctrine of the Resurrection of the body came late into the mainstream of Jewish thought. It appears in a few late passages in the Old Testament and was believed in by many Jews of the first century, mainly by the party or school known as the Pharisees. In the Gospel story, Jesus took the side of the Pharisees against the Sadducees—the high priestly party that collaborated with Rome—over this very issue. Bodily Resurrection came to be the official position of the church very early on.

But distortions crept in. When the first Christians affirmed belief in the Resurrection of the body, they were not saying they believed that a human body, once deceased, would literally, particle by particle, be resuscitated one day. What they meant was that in the realm of "the age to come," in "heaven" or "on the other side," we will not be disembodied, gibbering shades or ghosts—like the dead of Homer's Hades or the Hebrew Sheol. The resurrected body was not to be a physical or material reality but something entirely new: a spiritual or transfigured body. Egyptian religion before and during the Hellenistic period held a similar view.

A lot of often foolish thinking and preaching about both the Resurrection of Jesus and the Resurrection of the rest of us could be avoided if the kind of distinction Paul sharply makes between corpses and spiritual bodies (I Cor. 15) was to be truly studied and taken to heart.

To recapitulate: Christian belief in the Resurrection of the body is based on belief in "a bodily rising from the dead" in the sense that with our new "spiritual bodies" we will recognize one another, progress and live much more than purely spectral or wraithlike lives. With such an understanding, worries over cremation of the physical body or the recovery of corpses after explosions or all other types of disaster where bodies are never found can be laid to rest.

Similarly, all literalistic fears and horrors over some sadistic, eternal punishment by searing flames of fire can finally be seen for the lurid metaphors they really are. Using the witness of those who have had near-death experiences, there could well be, in extreme cases, inner pain as we endure a life review or self-judgment in the presence of the Light on the other side. This will be a psychic or spiritual suffering as we are confronted with the kind of people we have been or the harm we have really done. Rather than last for a cruel eternity, this pain will last (if one can speak of time in this context beyond time) but a moment as it is swallowed up in the fire of God's love for each and every one.

This present, physical body of ours has a tremendous importance. We are all shrines or temples of the divine. As Paul reminds us: "We have this treasure in earthen vessels" (literally, clay pots). So, it matters very much what we do to and with our body, but it's not going with us when we go.

Frequently, we use the word "eternal" in speaking of life in the next dimension. This concept, too, has been a source of much bewilderment. The idea of some form of life that goes on forever and ever is not really all that appealing to everyone. It certainly isn't to me.

The Greek word in the New Testament translated as "eternal"— *aionios*—means "belonging to the age to come." It is not a time word but a qualitative word. Yes, it will be immortality. But it will be a totally different quality or kind of living: a nowness, an intensity, a fullness of being alive we have only glimpsed in rare moments of love, or music, or other beauty here "below." We won't be idle, as some fear, but learning, growing, co-working with God while discovering the reasons for our existence.

With you, I will want to know for starters: Why does God allow suffering, and was the gift of free will to us something the Spirit now regrets?

NON-CHRISTIAN WRITERS MADE
NO MENTION OF HISTORIC JESUS

Whenever, as in Chicago recently on a late-night, open-line show, there is a discussion of my thesis that there may well never have been an historical Jesus of Nazareth, inevitably the challenger brings up a quotation from the Roman historian Tacitus (55–120 C.E.).

He is the first pagan to mention the execution of "Christus." In his Annals (Book 15, chapter 44) written in or about the year 115, he writes how Emperor Nero, in order to shift blame for having set fire to a large part of Rome—to make way for his own architectural schemes—accused "a class of men loathed for their vices whom the crowd called Christians." By itself, this only illustrates what has been said here about there being groups of worshippers of a spiritual Christ in various Mediterranean communities before and during the first century. The short statement that follows, however, is the one most quoted by upholders of a historic Jesus.

Tacitus says: "Christus, the founder of the name, had been executed in the reign of Tiberius, by sentence of the procurator, Pontius Pilate." It is largely on these few words that the whole case for a Jesus of history rests. It undergirds the credal assertion: "He suffered under Pontius Pilate and was crucified."

Tacitus gives no source for this affirmation and it is unlikely, given the thousands of victims crucified throughout the vast empire, that any official records were kept. Thus, while scholars are divided, it seems most probable that he was repeating hearsay. Some commentators suggest that since Tacitus doesn't appear to have been in the habit of consulting original documents, he was simply repeating rumours heard in Rome or in the province of Asia, which he had governed a few years before writing his Annals.

New Testament scholar Norman Perrin, in his Introduction to
the New Testament, notes that Tacitus's information was "probably
"based upon police interrogation of Christians." Professor G. A.
Wells (*Did Jesus Exist?*) asserts that Tacitus is not an "independent
witness"; he is merely repeating what some Christians had by then
come to believe.

What is significant historically is that even in giving this terse
summary of a presumed event, Tacitus gets his facts wrong. He calls
Pilate the "procurator" of Judea. This was the title used for provin-
cial governors in the second century when he is writing. But it is not
what governors of Judea were called in or around 33 to 35 C.E. The
official term at that time was "prefect" of Judea.

The host of the talk show then raised another extremely brief
and ambiguous passage used to bolster the historical Jesus position.
The Roman historian Suetonius (75–160 C.E.), in his *The Lives of
the Caesars*, seemingly refers to Christians in this brief passage:
"Claudius expelled from Rome the Jews who, under the influence
of Chrestus, did not cease to cause trouble."

Chrestus was a popular name at the time and simply means "a
good man." Was he then some unknown Jewish fanatic or trouble-
maker? Or, in this instance, is it rather a case of bad spelling on
Suetonius's or his source's part? Are the agitators perhaps Messianic
Jews hoping for a Christ-figure to come? Is the Chrestus cited actu-
ally there on the scene or merely the object of his followers' beliefs?
Are these in all probability followers of the mythic Christ to whom
I have already referred?

I agree with scholars who conclude that the whole passage is
too plagued with uncertainties and vagueness to be solid evidence of
anything. The same can be said of the well-known reference by Pliny
the Younger in a letter to Emperor Trajan in or about the year 112 C.E.
Pliny was serving as governor of Bithynia in Asia Minor and he writes
Trajan for counsel on how tough he should be on Christ-worshippers
who refuse to pay homage to traditional gods and the emperor.

He writes that they meet "regularly before dawn" and chant verses
in honour of Christ "as to a god" and then later meet to consume

food "of an ordinary, harmless kind." Pliny reports that even under torture he found "nothing but a degenerate sort of cult carried to extravagant lengths."

Again there is no mention at all of any Jesus of Nazareth as an historical person. In fact, Pliny leaves the reader in total darkness as to whether the Christ being worshipped was historical or mythical.

The last non-Christian testimony to alleged historicity also came up in the Chicago discussion. The host and my friendly "opponent"—a church-history professor from a Catholic college in Chicago—brought up the famous passage from the Jewish historian Flavius Josephus. That, as we shall see next, provides even less solid support for historicity than the few lines already cited above.

PROOF OF HISTORIC JESUS OR
JUST CLEVER FORGERY?

Edward Gibbon, author of *The Decline and Fall of the Roman Empire*, was not, as is well known, an admirer of Christianity as far as its account of its earliest origins are concerned. Known for his "meticulous accuracy," he refused to take seriously any church history until about 250 C.E. because he found such a mass of forgeries and deceit in the earlier period.

He wrote: "The scanty and suspicious materials of ecclesiastical history seldom enable us to dispel the dark cloud that hangs over the first age of the church." Elsewhere he comments: "The most extravagant legends, as they conduced to the honour of the Church [sic], were apprehended by the credulous multitude, countenanced by the power of the clergy, and attested by the suspicious evidence of ecclesiastical history."

Gibbon's views are relevant because while the Jesus Christ of the mythos will live forever, the "Jesus of history" is the focus of intense debate. Gibbon boldly calls the lone, seemingly solid piece of non-Christian evidence for an historical Jesus from the first century "an example of no vulgar forgery," that is, the forgery was deliberately, obviously and astutely concocted by one who knew fully what he was doing.

He was referring to probably the most keenly contested passages in all antiquity, the so-called Testimonium Flavianum by the historian Josephus. Several modern New Testament scholars—for example, John P. Meier, who in *A Marginal Jew* said its importance is "monumental"—have gone so far as to admit that without the authenticity of Josephus's testimony, there is no "proof" of the existence of Jesus at all. Not a line of the Gospels can be confirmed without it.

Flavius Josephus (37–100 C.E.) was a Jewish writer, a Pharisee, and ultimately a loyal friend of Rome. Here is the disputed passage with the boldly "Christian" parts in italic:

> At this time there appeared Jesus *a wise man if indeed one should call him a man.* For he was a doer of startling deeds, a teacher of people who receive the truth with pleasure. And he gained a following both among many Jews and among many of Greek origin. *He was the Christ.* And when Pilate, because of an accusation made by the leading men among us, condemned him to the cross, those who had loved him previously did not cease to do so. *For he appeared to them on the third day, living again, just as the divine prophets had spoken of these and countless other wondrous things about him.* And up to this present day the tribe of Christians, named after him, has not died out.

The italicized words were recognized as suspect years before Gibbon, but today, Meier, along with many conservative scholars, offers a shortened version which deletes the openly Christian phrases and so attempts to make Josephus an acceptable witness for critics.

Thus his reply to Gibbon is that he is only partly right. There is still a solid substratum of evidence upon which to base the case for the historic Jesus. The "revised" version then reads:

> At this time there appeared Jesus, a wise man. He was a doer of startling deeds, a teacher of people who receive the truth with pleasure. And he gained a following both among many Jews and among many of Greek origin. And when Pilate, because of an accusation made by the leading men among us, condemned him to the cross, those who had loved him previously, did not cease to do so. And up until this very day the tribe of Christians, named after him, has not died out.

Ideally, one would check the accuracy of this account by directly consulting the copies of Josephus's histories in the possession of the contemporary Jewish authorities. But by a mysterious quirk, matching the fate of other (usually pagan) writings inimical to the Christian cause, these are among the many documents written by Jews in the period between 200 B.C.E. and 200 C.E. that went wholly missing. They were only transmitted to the Jews later by the Christians.

There are two very compelling reasons for dismissing this shorter version also as wholly bogus. Josephus's writings are marked throughout by his extreme hostility to any and every Messianic Jew executed by the Romans. To call Jesus a "wise man" and a "teacher of the truth" is totally out of character for him. It would also mean that he is openly accusing Pilate of having executed such an exemplary man. This jars completely with his clear aim of always ingratiating himself with his superiors. He was a Roman citizen and what is more, a pensioned client of the Flavians.

However, the clincher is that despite its obvious usefulness in Christian polemics—say, for Origen contra Celsus, his Pagan opponent, or for Justin Martyr or Irenaeus in their debates with critics, Jewish and pagan—no church authority quotes this passage until the fourth century. Significantly, Eusebius (died 359) quotes it first, and all the evidence points to him as the forger.

PAUL SHOWED LITTLE INTEREST
IN ANY HISTORICAL JESUS

The Apostle Paul pops up in the media from time to time. Usually, except where his famous Damascus road conversion is used as a metaphor for any sudden turnaround wherein a celebrity "sees the light" and abruptly switches careers, lifestyles or partners, Paul generally, however, gets bad press. Some theologian, or perhaps a novelist, for example, comments on his alleged anti-sex, anti-female, anti-all-who-don't-agree-with-him biases.

What seldom, if ever, gets coverage is the utter mystery of his relationship with, or knowledge of, an historical Jesus of Nazareth. Paul preserves a virtual silence on this topic—something preachers never mention.

In his Letter to the Galatians, he says he learned of the Good News from a direct "revelation" of Jesus Christ, a purely inner, spiritual event. He takes trouble to argue that he owed nothing to anybody else in this "for I never received it of anyone neither was taught it." Immediately after his stunning, paranormal vision on the road to Damascus (obviously not an encounter with an historical, actual person), he tells how he went to the wilds of Arabia and stayed away (reflecting and reading no doubt) for a full three years.

Then, he says he returned, went up to Jerusalem and spent fifteen days with Peter. What did they talk about? Since he had never in real life encountered or known what he calls "a Jesus after the flesh," one would think the time would have been spent learning all he could about the supposed founder of Christianity. What did he really look like? What and how did he teach? What did he do?

Were there any miracles? Where was he killed and buried? Where was his tomb? In short, where and when did it all happen?

In posing such questions remember one key fact. There were no Gospels yet in existence. Mark didn't appear until after 70 C.E. Paul's letters, dating from about 50 to 60 C.E., are the earliest material in the New Testament. Whenever Paul mentions Scripture—his Bible—he means the Hebrew Bible. All he could hope to rely on was the remembered testimony of those who were reputed to be followers of this messiah. Peter was the key man to know, so to speak.

Yet the staggering truth is evident to all who take the trouble to investigate for themselves that Paul appears to have little interest in an historical Jesus. He never refers to him as Jesus of Nazareth; he never repeats a single parable, miracle or other deed of the Master except for the words ascribed to Jesus in instituting the Last Supper or Eucharist. However, notice that in introducing this passage he reminds the reader that what he repeats is what he "received of the Lord." Clearly, he is referring again to some mystical revelation from a heavenly or spiritual entity and not to any historical encounter in the natural world. The words are standard material from a Mystery-type religion.

Yes, he once describes Jesus Christ as "born of a woman," but this was also true of some of the other saviour figures of the Mystery Religions in the surrounding culture, for example, Osiris and Horus. None of these was considered to have been historical. In fact, to put the strongest piece of negative evidence out directly, Paul tells his readers on another occasion (II Cor. 5:16) that he had made a conscious decision henceforth not to know Christ "after the flesh," that is, in a normal, human manner, but as Lord of glory. He seems to be chiding those who wanted to cling to a historicized version of the story.

The puzzle becomes acute in those parts of his letters where it would have served his argument enormously to have been able to quote an apt, pithy saying of Jesus, to cite a specific parable or at least refer to some precedent from the kind of picture later given in the four Gospels.

For example, it would have greatly pitched and enhanced this point that Resurrection is a reality, as he wrestles to do in I Corinthians 15, had he been able to cite the raising of Lazarus described in John's Gospel, or the empty tomb of Easter. But he knows nothing of these or indeed of other raisings of the dead by Jesus or the mind-boggling Resurrections recorded in Matthew's account of Jesus' crucifixion when nearby tombs opened and many of the saints allegedly "arose" and walked into Jerusalem (chapter 27:52–3). He says nothing of a virgin birth either.

The case is cumulative and the "argument from silence" always has critics. But I believe the evidence shows a picture of a man whose religion bears very little resemblance to the cult of the personal Jesus so widely prevalent in North America today. Paul doesn't speak much of an historical Jesus because he knew of none. His Jesus Christ, then, is the mystical, universal Christos of all the ages.

Paul's faith was purely spiritual, a matter of daily experiencing the Spirit of God indwelling his heart and mind.

ST. PAUL SAW

RESURRECTION AS A METAPHOR

Some of my newspaper column's most avid readers seem to have a limited view of who or what constitutes "a real Christian." Consequently, they write caustically stating why they believe I belong "outside the camp." Fortunately, few things could matter less—as long as these exclusivists keep reading and thinking. But sometimes there's an irony. This is the case when, as often happens lately, they say that I cannot be a genuine Christian unless I believe literally— among other things—that Jesus was raised "physically" from the dead. In other words, unless you commit to the "physical Resurrection" of an historical Jesus, you are beyond the pale of Christianity.

This judgment puts so many of us in such early and renowned Christian company—those who had minds well beyond the learning or brilliance today's theologians dare to claim. Take, for example, St. Clement of Alexandria (150–215 C.E.) and his mightier pupil, Origen (185–254 C.E.). Both took the allegorical/spiritual approach to scripture and would have been really shocked to see the way today's "Christianism" so often distorts the original spiritual reality.

Interestingly, however, there is another being tried with us on this issue, one weightier still than any church father or other biblical exegete. I refer to that great "lion" of the faith, St. Paul himself. Paul couldn't be clearer, in his oft-quoted peroration in I Corinthians 15 on the Resurrection of the dead, that Jesus' Resurrection—and hence our own one day—was categorically and supremely a spiritual "event." He's so insistent on this, goes to such great lengths to expatiate upon it and thunders it home with such eloquence that it's truly astounding how would-be Bible champions can read it and not comprehend its meaning. The passage is pure Platonism throughout.

Don't take my word alone. Let's look at it. As the chapter opens, Paul quotes the tradition handed on to him how various people "saw" the risen Lord and says that lastly the Christ was seen by him "as of one born out of due time" (a reference to his later, unusual Damascus road experience). Significantly, the Greek verb he uses to describe his own "seeing," *opthe,* is the one he uses to describe the sightings by the others. But it's a technical term, widely used in the popular Mystery Religions of the day, to denote a paranormal, psychic vision. Paul is decidedly not talking here about ordinary physical sight at all.

Move on then to verse 35 and following where he actually discusses and answers the legitimate, pressing question: "How are the dead raised up?" His argument is a little tortured, but if you stick with it he makes the same point repeatedly: What goes into the ground at death is definitely not what moves on to the dimension of eternal life or the life of "the age to come." What goes into the grave is corporeal, physical, eminently corruptible. What comes out is immortal, spiritual through and through. As the old Egyptians said: The body to earth; the soul to heaven.

Paul uses the old metaphor of sowing a seed. Those who have planted seed potatoes and then encountered the rotting remains afterwards while harvesting new potatoes can identify with his point. You don't "sow" that which comes up. "God giveth it a (new) body."

Paul says plainly that this describes the Resurrection of the dead, Jesus' and ours, for they are identical: "It is sown in corruption; it is raised in incorruption. It is sown a natural (or physical) body, it is raised a spiritual body. There is a natural body and there is a spiritual body . . . and as we have borne the image of the earthly, we shall also bear the image of the heavenly."

In case this is not completely transparent, he then lays it down as emphatically as possible: "Now this I say . . . flesh and blood cannot inherit the kingdom of God; neither doth corruption inherit incorruption . . . we shall all be changed!" Our decay-prone bodies—"this corruptible"—shall put on "incorruption," and that which is so clearly mortal "will put on" immortality. This leads him to that classic cry so often repeated at funerals: "Death, where is thy sting? O grave, where is thy victory?"

Paul, whose genuine epistles date much earlier than the Gospels, from c.50 to 60 C.E., never mentions an empty tomb. Why not? He knew nothing of it. For him, the Resurrection was an entirely spiritual matter. He knew nothing of the later Resurrection stories in the Gospels about Jesus eating fish or walking about talking to fishermen. All of that was added as the demand for a more literalistic, made-for-the-lowest-common-denominator version imposed itself upon the original story. True, he lists apparent "sightings" of the Risen Christ at the outset of I Corinthians 15. But, significantly, these do not accord at all with the much later stories in the Gospels, and clearly, from the language used, denote visionary phenomena similar to those of the Mystery Religions or certain Gnostic groups. They are striking in their total lack of all the ingredients essential for history, that is, any specific indication of either place or time.

FAITH IS AN INNER RECOGNITION
OF A TRUTH TOO DEEP FOR WORDS

The Buddha is believed to have lived from approximately 563 to 483 B.C.E. In other words, he was reputed to have been born roughly six centuries before the baby of Bethlehem. Yet, the earliest written account of what Joseph Campbell and other comparative-religion scholars call "the myth of the Buddha" is in what is known as the Pali Canon. It was first set down in Ceylon some five centuries later and about eight hundred kilometres distant from its birthplace in India.

Campbell says, in a carefully measured understatement, that "it is not likely that it is a very accurate biography nor in any way the kind that a modern biographer would wish to have achieved." As I pointed out in the previous piece, much the same can be said of the Jesus of the Christian Gospels.

In a remarkable way, the stories of the Buddha's birth, life and teachings show close parallels with those of Jesus. So, of course, do those of the Hindu Lord Krishna and other saviour figures of the past. The basic mythos or story being told is really a fundamental archetype in the human psyche. I believe it was planted there by the Ground or Mind of the Universe, that is, by the awesome mystery we call God.

The fact that none of this is historical in a modern, secular sense in no way detracts from or destroys the enormous spiritual potency and inner truth of the overall message being conveyed. For example, to be quite personal, the power and meaning of my own Christian beliefs are in no way affected by the reality of questioning Jesus' historicity. On the contrary, the Jesus Story and the truth it carries for the soul and for the world became much more comprehensible and relevant for me once the weight of always trying to sort out the impossibilities and contradictions of a more literal, historicized understanding was lifted from my shoulders.

While fully appreciating the vision of life's meaning, of ethical behaviour, and of the divine witnessed to by other world faiths, I remain a Christian. I do so not just because that is the "rock out of which I was hewn," but because I have come to see more deeply how a rational understanding of Christianity's essentially mystical message transforms one's outlook on oneself, one's fellow human beings and the entire cosmos.

Expressed in allegory, parable, poetry and wisdom sayings, the Jesus Story is the dramatic telling of the story of every life on the one hand and of the divine compassion of the Creator towards us on the other.

There are at least these two levels to the account. One is the supremely moving tale of God's love poured out on our behalf. The other is the depiction of the Christ principle or divine spark hidden in every heart—waiting to be discovered, fanned into open flame, and ultimately to glow in glory. This is indeed what the Apostle Paul called the ultimate mystery, "Christ in you, the hope of glory."

When I say such a faith is rational, I mean that to hold it means one need never be afraid of questioning, of moving outside the box, of facing up to any intellectual challenge. Reason is God's greatest gift to us and we are meant to love God "with all your mind," as well as with heart and strength—our entire being.

When I say this faith is mystical, there is no sense whatever of anything spooky, emotional or far-out. It is not irrational but rather non-rational. It's an intuitive, inner recognition of truth that is often too deep for words. It's a becoming aware, as Yeshua or Jesus says in the Gospel of Thomas, that the kingdom, or presence, of God is all about us even though often "the people see it not." Or, as Jesus says in Matthew's Gospel, one recognizes that the kingdom or the Christ consciousness is "within you."

This is a faith that opens one up to what I call a "cosmic spirituality." It enables one to view the whole of the universe as the word of God, that is, as the manifestation of the divine Mind or Logos in and through everything from a bubbling brook to a humming-bird's flight, from T. S. Eliot's "hidden laughter of children in the foliage" to the farthest, misty galaxies, from the highest mountains to the inner workings of the human brain.

But it is a faith that also enables one to see the Christ, the Imago Dei, the atman or holy soul in every other single human being on the planet of every or no religion, of every colour, tongue or political persuasion. I believe with St. Paul that with such a faith "all things are yours." To use Jesus' words, you "inherit the earth" and find indeed that all things have become new.

SYMBOLS ARE ALL ABOUT REALITY

Earlier, I argued strongly for a mythical-allegorical understanding of the Christian Gospels and the stories they tell. I also said New Testament scholarship has been on the wrong scent trying to track down "historical" nuggets in the Jesus Story; that the way to go is to understand the complete account as a "divine drama where Jesus, as the persona representing the Christ of the universal myth" does and says the same things all ancient saviour figures in the various Mystery Religions did and said.

Does saying something or someone is "symbolic" mean that it or he/she is "unreal" or disconnected from reality? Is an allegorical and metaphorical story simply a fairy tale or worse? Is it really "debunking" Christianity to say its central tale is a sublime myth?

A letter from a bright atheist notes that I frequently try to combat the current tide of biblical literalism by expounding the symbolic nature of all "God talk," especially in the sacred literature of world religions. He gives this effort a nod of approval since he finds the statements made by religious literalists to be often "ludicrous and contradictory."

However, he makes this rather ludicrous statement himself. He writes: "I have no specific grief with symbols. They work as teaching aids and expression tools but we both know they are not statements of reality." Because he holds such a view, he goes on to say he finds it "fascinating" that we seem to share many of the same premises but have come to widely divergent conclusions. I remain a firm believer; he, an atheist. Then he says: "Quite frankly, I don't see why you still believe. Faith cannot be the answer. You are too logical for that old excuse." He closes with his "open-minded willingness" to be persuaded otherwise and his appreciation of my willingness "to go beyond a purely Christian perspective." He closes: "Every week I learn something."

You may be interested in the essence of my reply to him. The matters at stake are weighty, not just for the agnostics and atheists who regularly read and react to the column but for the general public as well. Few areas of knowledge and of spirituality in particular are surrounded by more misunderstanding than the subject at hand.

There are a hundred reasons, logically, rationally and also intuitively, that I am a believer. This is not the time to expatiate on them. Here the focus is on symbolism and its alleged unreality. The truth is that symbols, metaphors and allegories have everything to do with reality. To dismiss them as mere fiction or, as another reader recently wrote, "the equivalent of lies," is sheer ignorance or lack of thought.

Think about it. A wedding ring is of itself merely a circle of precious metal, but it's a symbol of a mighty reality. It is not of itself love, commitment, fidelity, marriage or family, but it can powerfully represent all of these and more. Its potency is far beyond all proportion to its commercial value or beauty.

Life is surrounded by, and only made possible by, symbols and symbolism, from the world of advertising to quantum physics and the various grades of mathematics. More obvious even still is the fact of human language. All words are symbols. It's what they stand for and the power they represent and convey that's so important. Life is virtually impossible without them. That's why poet Ralph Waldo Emerson could boldly say: "A good symbol is the best argument, and is a missionary to persuade thousands." You just have to think of Winston Churchill during the Second World War flashing his cocky V-for-victory symbol with upraised fingers to know the truth of Emerson's insight.

American educator John Dewey, in *The Quest For Certainty*, writes: "The invention or discovery of symbols is doubtless by far the greatest single event in the history of man. Without them no advance is possible; with them there is no limit set to intellectual development except inherent stupidity." But since people are more open to being convinced by science rather than theology or philosophy, here's the scientist Sir James Jeans. *In The World Around Us*, he says: "When we try to discuss the ultimate structure of the atom, we are driven to speak in terms of similes, metaphors, and parables."

It's exactly the same when humans try to speak of the things of God.

JESUS IS THE MEDIUM
WHO BECAME ESSENTIAL MESSAGE

———————

Everybody, religious or not, talks about the Ten Commandments as though they know what they are but, in fact, very few could list them apart from not killing, not stealing and not committing adultery.

This is unfortunate because the other seven "shalt nots" are just as important as these; in fact, the first one, according to the Bible, is the greatest of all: "You shall have no other gods before me" (Exodus 20:1). Notice in passing that this passage acknowledges that there are other gods; however, they are not to be worshipped. Then there is the commandment about not creating any kind of idol in place of Yahweh (no. 2).

Why stress these first two commandments? The issue is crucial, though some could find what follows disturbing. It comes, however, with the full backing of not just the verses already cited but the rest of the biblical witness, both the Old and New Testaments.

Given the clear stand of the Scriptures against putting anything or anyone in the place of God, it's evident that the orthodox teaching of the Christian church continues to be in a position of total disobedience and betrayal. Taking a first-century Jewish peasant man, Jesus, whose historicity is now in serious dispute (see, for example, *The Jesus Myth* by G. A. Wells), later defined at Chalcedon as "fully human, fully divine," has put him in a central position in the place of the Almighty and has worshipped him as God himself.

No alien visitor to a Christian church on Easter Day, for example, particularly if it is conservative (but by no means are liberal churches excluded), can miss the overwhelming central presence of Jesus everywhere in the prayers, hymns and preaching. It is one of the clearest examples of the medium of a message having become the essential message itself that I have encountered in a lifetime of observation.

Put absolutely and as starkly as possible: Christianity thus is guilty of a staggering act of idolatry—one which, ironically, the Jesus portrayed in the Gospels would have utterly repudiated. After all, when challenged by his enemies to cite the greatest commandment in the Torah, the Mosaic Law, he (Mt.22:37) promptly replied it was: Love of God with all of one's heart, soul, and mind—and of one's neighbour as oneself. That is the answer one would expect from any devout, orthodox Jew both then and now.

When the wealthy young man of Mark's Gospel (10:17) came running, knelt at his feet and said: "Good Teacher, what must I do to inherit eternal life?" Jesus instantly told him off. He chided: "Why do you call me good? Nobody is good except God alone."

Even the Fourth Gospel, that of John, which has the "highest" view of Jesus' person, maintains a strict subordination of status. Jesus prays to the Father; he says that anything he teaches the disciples comes directly from the Father, that is, God. Nowhere does he ever categorically claim to be God. Some of the Church of England's most noted scholars, even though considered conservative overall, have admitted as much.

When it comes to the Acts of the Apostles and the letters of St. Paul, it is clear that at all levels of understanding, literal or metaphorical, Jesus is always totally subordinate to God.

His Resurrection is not something he—as many Easter hymns wrongly clarion—does by himself, bursting forth from the tomb. Text after text makes it clear that "God raised him from the dead"— not physically, but, as Paul makes plain in I Corinthians 15:44, "spiritually." The original Greek is clear. He did not rise from the dead. He was raised up by an act of the "Father."

Few people reciting the creeds each Sunday in the various denominations are aware that it took the church a long drawn-out process—until the Council of Chalcedon in the middle of the fifth century C.E.—to work out finally how the man Jesus could be fully incorporated into a Trinitarian formula where he ends up with the same nature (Greek *homoousios*) or essence as the Father.

In the nearly five centuries that it took for all this to happen, all thinkers, Bible exegetes and others who quarrelled with the emerging and admittedly Byzantine logic employed by the prevailing orthodoxy were systematically denounced, persecuted or killed. Their books were burned, their academies closed and their names anathematized.

As Elaine Pagels has pointed out in her studies of early Gnosticism—one of the main dissenting movements—we have been left with only the story and the position of the winning side.

Sadly, the mistaking of the medium for the message in the case of Christianity has had terrible, bloody consequences down the ages, particularly in relationships with two other major world faiths, Judaism and Islam. Both Judaism and Islam hold that Christianity took a tragic and fateful turn towards idolatry in the late third, fourth and fifth centuries. The evidence shows that critique to be correct.

CHOPPING UP THE FROZEN SEA INSIDE US

I think we ought to read only the kind of books that
wound and stab us. . . . We need the books that affect us
like a disaster, that grieve us deeply. . . . A book
must be the axe for the frozen sea inside us.
— FRANZ KAFKA (1884–1924)

This quotation describes with uncanny precision the kind of books
I researched before writing *The Pagan Christ*. Naturally, such books
inevitably shock, offend and often acutely anger those most deeply
invested in the status quo. Those with most to lose begin to feel the
ground shaking under their feet as the ice-breaking message comes
forth. But such books also carry with them the seeds of great hope
for a future of expanded consciousness and personal progress for
those prepared to grapple with new and radical ideas.

Obviously, *The Pagan Christ* has struck a chord in the hearts of
a large and growing number of people, with many writing moving
letters telling of spiritual liberation. Obviously, too, it has provoked
Christian proselytizers and conservatives of many stripes to attack
and do all in their power to discredit or weaken the book's credibil-
ity. This, in the light of Kafka's words, was entirely predictable.
Some of the tactics and language used by the book's detractors have
been unfortunate in view of their authors' claims to orthodox
Christian beliefs. But, again, this is not surprising because so much
is at stake for them.

Significantly, the critics always try to undermine one's sources
even though none to date has shown any sign of having taken the
effort to read them themselves. Many of the criticisms circle about

footnotes and other peripheral issues while avoiding the central thrust of the book's message.

While the question of whether Jesus was an historical person is not the key point being made—I find, and have already argued in some detail, the evidence for historicity sadly lacking—it has dominated a lot of the controversy since the book's publication. Since much of the fuss has been filled with unhappy distortions, it may be helpful to deal with the most salient one here.

Contrary to what is said, it should be made quite clear that I am far from being alone among scholars who today view the so-called historical Jesus with total skepticism. True, most scholars of the California-based Jesus Seminar retain a very "minimalist historical Jesus," but those familiar with their work know they have now peeled this particular "onion" down to such a fine core that it is barely discernible.

There is no talk of any Resurrection, for example. I recommend in this connection two books by Jesus Seminar fellow Dr. Robert M. Price: *Deconstructing Jesus* and *The Incredible Shrinking Son of Man*. Price is professor of biblical criticism at J. Colemon Theological Seminary, Carol City, Florida.

For a truly thorough-going—and I believe wholly convincing—examination of the problem, one could read the seven books by Professor G. A. Wells, now retired from London University in the U.K. Among the titles are *The Jesus Myth* and *Did Jesus Exist?* His most recent work, *Can We Trust the New Testament?*, is, arguably, the best survey of all the current scholarly research in this field.

Wells quotes, for example, from the scholarly writings of the present Archbishop of Canterbury, Rowan Williams, on the alleged sightings of the Risen Christ in the four Gospels: ". . . a monumentally confused jumble of incompatible stories" the conflict among which has never been "satisfactorily sorted out" and all of which "bear the marks of extremely sophisticated literary editing."

Williams calls the "amazement" of the disciples over the alleged Resurrection "a literary convention" and goes on to say that what the Easter texts present are "imaginative approaches" in the form of stories.

The archbishop notes that the only "early testimony" is Paul's list in I Corinthians 15 but adds reluctantly that it doesn't correlate with the Gospel appearances and is a mere list with no indication whatever of the time, place or circumstances. Thus the vaunted evidence for a literal Resurrection calls for a leap of blind faith. It falls apart on closer examination.

The most serious difficulty to be faced on historicity is, as we have seen, the total absence of anything that can be called hard secular evidence for an historical Jesus coming out of the entire first century apart from Christian-sourced writings. In a day and age when there were secular (pagan) historians, satirists and other observers in abundance, none saw fit to record any of the miracles or bizarre supernatural phenomena—such as the eclipse of the sun during the crucifixion or the earthquake or the opening of the tombs and appearances of the dead described in Matthew. The only reference to Jesus of Nazareth, by Josephus, is a clear forgery from the fourth century.

The historical Jesus is vanishing. The spiritual Christ within awaits our discovery.

CAN A VIBRANT RELIGION EXIST
WITHOUT AN ACTUAL FOUNDER?

———————

There is a widespread, vigorously held assumption that the powerful religious movement that came to be known as Christianity must have had an historical figure as its founder and initiator. This personage is generally assumed to have been a Jewish peasant-turned-prophet called Jesus of Nazareth.

Conservative scholars believe that he was the Son of God, a literal God-man, "from the foundation of the world." He proved this, they contend, by his miracles and, in particular, by his death followed by his Resurrection some thirty-eight to forty hours later. (The "three days" is a stretching of the Gospel accounts.)

Liberal scholars such as those of the Jesus Seminar paint a different picture. According to them, he was a charismatic-type healer and preacher of social justice who ran afoul of the authorities and was crucified for it. His miracles and the Resurrection are whittled down or explained away completely. But such was his impact on his closest followers that they used him to reinterpret the Old Testament and gave him titles and powers that eventuated in the full-blown "wholly God wholly man" figure of fourth- and fifth-century orthodoxy.

Both camps agree that there was an historical core to the initial process, but each faces us with its own set of particular difficulties. If you follow the most strident group, you end up having to take the miracles and the entire supernatural framework literally. For many moderns, trained to regard intellect as God's greatest gift to humans, this requires mental leaps which, when fully acknowledged, render the project, quite simply, impossible. Like a beach ball held under water, the doubts surrounding such a faith ultimately must surface—

or be forced down, at great emotional and mental risk—and held under until they surface again.

Liberals, having stripped the story to its minimum, are left with not much to proclaim. There is little Gospel or good news in the story of a young Jewish man who was allegedly quick with words, had a keen social conscience, helped some people find healing of various ills but later came to an unfortunate ending. The idea that to know him you first have to remove layer after layer of later theological speculation is not the stuff of which creative, joyful living today can be cobbled together.

There is, however, a third way, that of taking the Gospels for the mythical creations they were and are and seeing the entire Jesus Story from a wholly spiritual perspective. Then the miracles can jump out at you with fresh relevancy and power. As Joseph Campbell put it so well: The myth always remains as "what never was (historically) but always is." It's the inner meaning that counts.

But the burning question is: Can there be a vibrant religion without an actual historic founder? Yes, as any study of comparative religions reveals, there can be indeed. My own view is that Christianity is a glowing example of this. Since that is the point at issue, however, we must turn our attention elsewhere.

What about the religion of Mithras? Many centuries old, it flourished in the first century and gave Christianity quite a competitive scare at times. It was especially popular among the soldiers in Caesar's armies. Mithraism had a god-man figure at its centre who was born in a cave and was accompanied by twelve followers (cowherds); its sacred meal and its baptisms paralleled the church's sacraments; its birth was accompanied by portents in the heavens. One Mithraeum inscription reads: "You saved us with the outpouring blood." But none of the followers of Mithras mistook him for an historical person. They at least knew the difference between myth and literalism.

Hinduism is another example of religions that do not have a specific founder. Some might argue it is more a philosophy than a religion, but the fact remains that the millions of Hindus today do not point to any one historical person as the founder of their faith. There are various gods and Christ-like figures in the pantheon of deities but, apart from the great Himalayan Rishis of the far-off past, no single human figure lends his name alone to this world faith.

How, then, did Christianity begin? Nobody, however learned, really knows for certain. We do know that there was a lot of heated expectation in Palestine before and just after the beginning of the Common Era that Joshua, the fabled hero of olden times, would soon return to lead the Jews to victory and freedom. Joshua is identical with Jesus (Yeshua). The name means "God saves." There may well have been Jewish mystery cults who thought of Joshua as God's anointed ("Christos" means just that). Hence they were devoted to Yeshua as Christos. In Greek, that would be Jesus Christ.

From the epistles in the New Testament, we learn there were often Christ-worshippers in various Mediterranean communities, for example, Rome, even before Paul visited and preached there. They thus formed the basis of the fledgling movement he was to fan into full flame. Read his letters for yourself. You will soon recognize that his is a spirituality of the heart. His "Christ" is the spirit of God within us all.

ALL RELIGIONS' SACRED SCRIPTURES
UNDERWENT SOME HUMAN EDITING

———————

Contrary to what millions of people believe, God is not in the publishing business. God does not write or produce books, however sacred they are and however highly they are esteemed by their followers. God does not speak Arabic, Hebrew, Greek, Latin, English or any language. Books are written by human beings. All books. At all times.

One can say special scriptures are the result of divine inspiration. But they are not the literal "words" or Word of God. God is Spirit, the New Testament says, and Spirit neither speaks nor writes any given tongue.

As a young man training for the Anglican ministry, I attended a college whose motto is *"Verbum Domini Manet,"* a quote from one of the Psalms. It means, the Word of the Lord abides (forever). It took me a while to ponder this and come to the awareness that much interpretation is required before these three words truly make sense. We can say metaphorically that God's word abides and that it is to be found in, say, the Bible or the Qur'an (Islam) or the Bhagavad-Gita (Hinduism), but beyond that we cannot go.

It soon became obvious to me, while still a fledgling student, that to take the entire Bible as "the Word of God" was morally and intellectually impossible. It was a moral impossibility because much of what the Bible contains utterly contradicts its own message of justice, compassion and mercy. Read the Book of Joshua for examples of genocide in the name of the Lord!

Moreover, it was impossible intellectually because the more one studied it the more obvious it became that a vast amount of human editing and recasting of old myths had gone on in its creation—

both Testaments. There are contradictions galore—not surprising in sixty-six different "books" written over a span of nearly a thousand years.

Once I had studied and learned Greek and could read the New Testament in a properly edited text with indices under every page outlining the roughly 150,000 variant readings that have come down to us in the various manuscripts (many are insignificant but some are of huge importance), the idea that this was word for word the Word of God became wholly untenable.

Compare the ending of Mark's Gospel in the King James Version with a good modern translation, The New Revised Standard Version, and you'll find that the Gospel actually ends at verse 8 of the last chapter. What follows in the King James Version is bogus. In fact, there are two later endings that attempt to fill the gap, one long, one shorter. Both are forgeries if left without comment. Any original ending has been lost. These false ones are scribal attempts to escape the embarrassment of having the story end on a down note. The disciples "were afraid."

Multiple contradictions and errors abound. Mark's Gospel, for example, has Jesus send evil spirits into a herd of pigs, which then rush down a steep cliff into the sea and perish. However, the nearest sea or body of water of any kind was several miles away from Gadara where the described event occurred. Mark obviously (from other signs as well) had never set foot in Palestine.

We know the Gospels were highly edited from their own witness. See, for example, John 21:25. It reads, "There are also many other things that Jesus did; if every one of them were written down, I suppose the world itself could not contain the books that would be written." Apart from the colossal exaggeration, notice the writer admits to picking and choosing, that is, acting as an editor. There's one editorial criterion, "that you may come to believe," stated clearly in John 20: 31. In fact, if you are discerning and read chapters 20 and 21 consecutively, you'll realize instantly why scholars hold that chapter 21 is a later addition to the text. It's really a second conclusion.

Added to all of this is the problem of translation. The original story was in Aramaic, we are told, though, as literary critic Harold Bloom has noted, why none of Jesus' sayings was ever preserved in Aramaic is a major puzzle. When you translate Aramaic into Greek, there is an inevitable change of meaning. When you then translate that Greek into English, there is a further change of meaning still. Add to this that even if the original were the "infallible Word of God," all the translators would have to be infallible in their work as well!

Why does all this matter? Today, there are three principle world faiths possessing powerful, militant minorities who are wholly committed to the belief that their scriptures are the exact Word of God. Each has its own plans and agenda for Jerusalem, as what they believe will be the "End" is presumed to be drawing nigh.

The huge and perilous crisis this could well precipitate hinges on the fact that each of these faiths believes that the Temple Mount in Jerusalem belongs to their God and thus to them. Fundamentalist Christians, fundamentalist Jews and fundamentalist Muslims all have their own private, utterly clashing hopes for that spot. Nothing less than world peace is at stake.

.

3

OUR RITUALS
HAVE COSMIC LINKS

The heavens declare the glory of God . . .
— PSALM 19:1

BEGINNING A NEW YEAR

RENOVATION COULD SHAKE US
TO OUR FOUNDATIONS

Three times over the past twenty-three years, Susan and I have carried out major home renovations on as many different dwellings. Actually, others did the work while I tried to keep out of the way. I may be able to parse lines of Thucydides, Homer or the Vulgate, but fixing and building are not my strong points. I once volunteered to repair a kitchen tap by replacing the washer. Somehow it ended up with a geyser of water that reached the ceiling and drenched all else besides. After that I took early retirement from the handyman role. It was what is called in North American football "a forced option."

As anyone who has been there knows, home renovations, however conducted, are not for the faint-hearted. Each time we did them and the dust had settled, we solemnly vowed never again. Since home is where I have worked ever since leaving the post of religion editor for the *Toronto Star* in 1983 to freelance, I had to study and to write my columns and books through each of these minor cataclysms. I can still almost taste the drywall dust and the fine wood particles in the air day after day. The pounding of hammers and the whining of drills, assorted electrical saws, screwdrivers and sanders, combined with the seemingly never-ending consultations required over what was to go where, made creativity at times a hard-won, holy grail.

Awesome though the experience of renovating your home can be, in reality it pales beside a much more drastic, costly, far-reaching renewal or "reno" than that, the renovation—or, to put it far better, the transformation—of oneself. That's the deeper meaning beneath the stirrings of will and conscience that sound within us or surface suddenly at this cusp of the old year and the imminent eve of the new.

We may joke about our New Year's resolutions or lightly promise ourselves and others a full prism of good intentions without ever realizing the actual seriousness of what is at work here. There is in the profound depths of every soul, however muted, repressed or denied it may be, a yearning to be and to do, yes, and to talk, at a higher level than we ever have in the past.

Buried, sometimes very deeply, in the human heart is the God-given longing to rise above our present selves, to be different, more like a secret vision we have long held fast within. Each of us experiences this awareness in our own unique fashion, but it is well nigh universal. And my best conviction tells me that its strength is mounting in our time.

Behind the current, growing interest in and popularity of spiritual themes, there is something much more than mere faddishness or social chic. A tide, a groundswell of seeking for an infinitely wiser, more enlightened way in both private and public life is steadily rising around us. The inner realization that we can be other, better than we are, is matched by a collectively increasing knowledge that

as a race we must be or face a *Götterdämmerung* of social and inter-
national chaos. My sense is that this new surge of aspiration is being
felt at the core of major religious communities worldwide. One
prays that this is so, since religions are so terribly involved in what
is going wrong.

This new surge of hope is not just a religious thing, thank God.
It's much wider than that. It's a prompting of the divine Spirit
within us all. The point is, however, to be *aware* that this is going
on and to nurture and foster it within and without. This means
facing up to the cost and the pain.

No renovation ever happens without some tearing down and
reconstruction. No personal transformation—and even, one day,
transfiguration—ever comes about without sacrifice and suffering.
People who dream that either they or this world will endure true
change without a price to be paid live still in a paradise for fools.
One cannot get from here to there without feeling the sculptor's
chisel. A little cosmetic rearranging—whether it be by the state, the
church, the synagogue, the temple, the mosque, your neighbour or
yourself—will be to no avail.

Too many individuals and institutions still believe that a deepening spirituality can be used to bolster the ego and the natural or
corporate self, thus bringing new power to the old order yet again.
This is delusional thinking. Transformation is about losing self and
its narrow, grasping, obsessive, controlling wiles and surrendering
to the Higher Self, to the divine within. This is the task to which
each of us is being called. May God give us all the listening ear and
the courage required to hear this still, small voice of opportunity
and challenge as never before.

SPRING

SPARKS OF COSMIC FIRE

Today around the world well over two billion people, or roughly two-thirds of all humanity, are celebrating Easter, the central festival of Christianity. Ideally, it is a time of feasting, unremitting joy and hope. Realistically, however, this occasion underlines persisting global divisions—for example, that the majority of living humans do not share this particular faith—and it takes place in an overall context of wars, rumours of wars, massive injustices, suffering and deep grief. No feasting, no joy, no hope.

There is a terribly urgent need, if our species is to advance even the smallest step on its upward evolutionary path, for an end to the real war that is behind all the other wars now raging or being contemplated by either sinister terrorist groups or smiling, would-be benign world leaders.

Spiritually speaking—and it goes to the very root of the matter—there is ultimately only one real war and that is the conflict going on at every moment in the heart of every individual on the planet. This is the "war" that the ancient sages saw as going on constantly in the unique phenomenon they recognized as being the crown of creation so far—the human organism.

This struggle is about reconciling the two aspects of our nature, our animal bodies and emotions and our divine mind-spirit-soul. From Plato to St. Paul, the message is clear. We are part animal, part god. Or, to quote the ancient philosopher Heraclitus, we are sparks of "cosmic fire" trapped in an earthly body but destined for the stars. That's why in the same newspaper one can read daily accounts of almost unimaginable human cruelty, wantonness and depravity on the one hand, and surpassing compassion, heroism, generosity, self-giving and sheer nobility on the other.

As one contemporary religious philosopher put it, the Battle of Armageddon is not some imaginary, future, apocalyptic battle but the moment-by-moment inner strife between greed, conceit, selfishness and lust for power and the higher desire to be more fully caught up in the divine flow. This microcosmic war within us is the war projected by our collective consciousnesses on the world screen beyond us and around.

Reflecting on this in the light of the message of Easter and the actualities of life at this hour, the question foremost in my mind is: "Is there not some universal story, some universal truth that is larger than the Christian Easter, the Jewish Passover, the Muslim Ramadan or any other specific, yet ultimately divisive, religious festival, however sacred?" Can our true unity as one-blood brothers and sisters on this one holy land which is the Earth itself be somehow made more visible, more intelligible, more real?

I believe the insights into our true nature just cited can help point the way. For example, if we could honestly say, with the inspired writer of these ancient lines, "I am a child of earth and of the starry sky, but my race is of heaven alone," we could hold on to our cherished religious tribalisms and at the same time transcend them with a profounder understanding of our single bond.

This is where comparative religions—the study of religious roots and commonalities—can be of enormous help. For example, the story of Jesus' suffering, crucifixion and Resurrection on the third day is part of dozens of ancient religions. The Egyptian god Osiris was killed and dismembered, only to be raised on the third day. The same is true of Dionysus, Orpheus and many others. Stories of divine deliverance such as that signified by the Passover belong to many others besides the Jews.

All of these much-loved accounts happen in the spring at or around the vernal equinox. There is a cosmic Resurrection, a cosmic Passover or deliverance being celebrated. It is the victory of light over darkness. The sun has finally triumphed over his "enemies."

This for the ancient theologians and philosophers was much more than nature symbolism. We are foolish if we suppose they worshipped the sun in itself. Rather, they saw in the movements of the natural world the garment and the "hand" of God. What's more, they saw it all as deeply about each one of us. The "victory" of the sun was the victory of your soul and mine—and the promise of immortality, a divine life to come.

If you can break old habits and just for once read the Easter narratives, or any of the great stories of the festivals celebrated by all faiths, not as descriptions of events that happened to another, or to many others long ago, but as the story of your own soul's journey, you'll come closer to what it's all about than ever before. We arrive here "trailing clouds of glory," and our destiny is "God who is our home."

FINAL VALUE OF ALL SPIRITUALITY
IS WHAT WE ARE AND WHAT WE DO

"Start blooming, frozen Christian!" challenged the medieval mystic Angelus Silesius. "Springtime is at hand. When will you ever bloom if not here and now!"

That is truly the message of this Easter and of any Resurrection to newness of life. The famous words of Silesius (1624–1677) are never far from mind: "Though Christ a thousand times in Bethlehem be born, / But not within thyself, thy soul will be forlorn; / The cross on Golgotha thou lookest to in vain / Unless within thyself it be set up again."

Coming alive again with joy is what all true religion is about. Thanks to my brother, Doctor George, dropping by for a brief visit last week and giving me a copy of *Living Buddha, Living Christ*, by Thich Nhat Hanh, the renowned scholar and mystic, I have been powerfully reminded of this truth we all know but so easily forget: that the final value of all spirituality, however sourced or named, is what we are and what we do. All the rest is an add-on. This can't be stated strongly enough.

If we are not more alive because of our faith, if we are not more compassionate, more awake and aware, more moved by the universal holy spirit of God that breathes in every single one of us, then all the anthems or hosannas today and all our theological correctness avail us nothing at all.

Silesius, who in his mystical and often controversial poems was greatly influenced by another holy man, Meister Eckhart, uses the potent analogy or metaphor of the dramatic explosion and renewal of nature every spring to call for each would-be believer's personal Resurrection.

No amount of sermonizing about the story of Jesus being raised up from the dead, no thundering arguments for any particular theory can ever replace the lived reality of knowing and showing that the same resurrecting spirit dwells in each of us. I firmly believe in the truth of a life, infinitely glorious, that shimmers on the other side of the transition we call death. Having studied this and researched it now for several decades, I find the constant, reductionist arguments of the skeptics and naysayers wholly wanting. No, it's not a matter of rewards and punishments; nor is it some atavistic fear of personal extinction. It's not some evolutionary benefit we've dreamed up to keep us toiling on.

Beneath the surface of the Gospel accounts of the Resurrection, with all their contradictions and problems, there flows a message as old as the race itself. The inner meaning of the Jesus Story this day is a major testimony to our immortality. We have sprung from other, spiritual dimensions of being, and to those we shall return.

Regular readers of my columns know that I am not given to swallowing unexamined or purely traditional "truths." I do not subscribe to the magical-thinking school of religion that believes in afterlife rewards selectively based on whether you accept or have "faith" that someone else long ago was "raised from the dead." Neither do I believe or accept the mental contortions some "experts" are prepared to go through in order to "prove" their dogmatic assumptions that the grave is the end and that's that. For example, the would-be debunkers of the near-death experiences (NDE) so familiar to everyone and witnessed everywhere by millions of people of all religions and of none never cease to amaze me with the lengths to which they're prepared to go in their debunking attempts. They try every futile argument: to wit, the whole thing is a product of anoxia or other changes in the brain when near death; it's a reliving of the birth process (!); it's a hallucination or some other imaginary projection, or whatever. Some have tried valiantly to reproduce an NDE by special helmets carrying electrical stimulation to specific parts of the brain.

Not one of dozens of such theories explains the deeply numinous, spiritually charged dimension of the real (as contrasted to induced) experience. None explains why an NDE is so life transforming. None accounts for flatliners (no brain waves at all) who nevertheless were aware of all that was going on around them.

But life here is what counts—now. On Easter Day, beyond all days, Christians have to ask themselves some serious questions. Why are religious people often so dishonest, mean and miserable? Why is theological hatred the most odious and virulent of human prejudices? How does ardent faith so often go together with a closed mind and a judgmental outlook on life? Do other people, regardless of their creed, colour, sexual orientation, visibly begin to wilt and wither in your presence, or, if you're aware enough, can you see that they feel a glow of empowering warmth in your presence and begin to blossom? As Silesius said: "Start blooming."

SUMMER

IN PRAISE OF STILLNESS

I was passing through London, England, once on an assignment elsewhere. I decided to use the time to try to arrange an interview with the Archbishop of Canterbury at the time, Most Reverend Michael Ramsey. Many will remember him, the quintessential archbishop, with longish white hair flowing from a dignified bald dome, a great craggy brow with fiercely thick eyebrows, and yet a face like a cherub. I had long admired his intellect and wisdom.

It turned out that the archbishop was involved in meetings at Brompton Oratory, so I hailed a cab and arrived there during a break for refreshments. Descending to the church basement with my trench coat still on, I spotted Archbishop Ramsey sitting at a table by himself with a teacup in front of him. Weaving through the crowd I began to introduce myself. But before I could say anything much, he picked up the cup and saucer and said, "How very kind of you. The tea urn is over there." So I got him a refill and, just as he gave me a nod of dismissal, managed to blurt out that I was a journalist and wanted to arrange an interview. His eyes twinkled and he said, "Don't count on it; don't count on it." That was it. His mind was elsewhere and my plans had to wait.

Eventually, on another trip, I did manage to talk to him. One thing he said stands out above the rest. Asked what he considered his major achievement, he said, "I think I have finally mastered the art of doing nothing." Aware of his books, his work and his busy life, I knew he didn't mean this in the sense of laziness or simply passing the time. He was talking about the art of creative, meditative sitting or being still. That was why, when called upon, he always had something significant to say. Those who run around a lot usually don't.

Reflecting on this, you realize that most of the truly creative leaps in history have begun when the innovators were "doing nothing." This is true of scientific breakthroughs—Isaac Newton under the apple tree, Archimedes in his bathtub, Einstein sitting on a streetcar, and so on, endlessly. It is true in the spiritual realm too—Jesus in the wilderness before the miracles began, Paul's vision while simply on the road to Damascus, St. Augustine while walking in a garden, or Muhammad in the mountain cave.

Some of the best books have been written when stillness and "doing nothing" were forced on the authors. Consider how many literary works have been forged and completed in prison. *Pilgrim's Progress* is an obvious example, but there have been scores of others, including parts of the New Testament, and in the modern era the letters of Dietrich Bonhoeffer. Viktor Frankl's moving book, *Man's Search for Meaning*, was born and written amidst the horror of a Nazi concentration camp. The late Bishop John Robinson once told me he wrote his best-known and most controversial book, *Honest To God*, in 1962 when he was hospitalized and confined to bed for several weeks with a complex leg injury. Every experienced farmer knows that the truly fertile field is one that regularly is allowed to lie fallow for a while "doing nothing."

Many today are searching for God. They run to this preacher or that guru, following the noise of the crowd and the slogans with the cleverest spin. But the reality itself eludes them. There's a marvellous story in the First Book of the Kings that speaks to this condition. Elijah the prophet had reached a low point in his life, so bad in fact that he prayed for death. He was being hunted down by Queen Jezebel, there was rampant apostasy and idolatry, and he felt utterly defeated and alone. God, too, he felt, had forsaken him. He went into the wilderness, and while he lay in a depressed and anxious sleep, "an angel touched him." He was told to make a journey to a cave on Mount Sinai. There, alone in that lunar-like remoteness, God gave him a fresh revelation. First there was a mighty wind that broke even rocks into pieces. "But the Lord was not in the wind." Then there was an earthquake followed by a consuming fire. But God was not in these either. Finally after all the noise and spectacle there was "a still, small voice," the assurance of the divine Presence with him and within. Incidentally, whereas he thought, like some people today, that he was the only one who stood for what was ethical and true, he was told there were "7,000 left in Israel" who had not "bowed the knee to Baal."

In today's world with its cacophony of urban roar and media info-bombardment there is more leisure but little real quietness. There are many who either from circumstances beyond their control or by choice have lots of time to do nothing. Yet they have no notion of true stillness. I would remind them of that most basic of all prayers: "Lord, teach me to sit still." Prayer is conversation with God. Too often the communication is all one way. We recite our needs. But it is in the stillness, if we listen, that we hear the voice of God. We can feel the divine "water" within us begin to flow and bubble up.

AUTUMN

IN AUTUMN, MORE IS GOING ON
THAN MEETS THE EYE

Endings are always beginnings. On Labour Day weekend, as the summer and the holidays wind up, North American culture girds itself for a fresh start—at school, at work and at every level of social activity.

Few of us give much thought, however, to how spiritually important the next few weeks are and how deeply what is going on at the surface level reflects the cycles of the heavens and the cosmos. Crucial for ancient, sage religion was this period leading up to and then following the approaching fall equinox of September 21. The sun, not just the source of all light and life on Earth, but also the most common and oldest of spiritual symbols known to us, is about to "stand still," momentarily as it were at the fall equinox, and then begin the slow descent to its own symbolic death and Resurrection.

It is no accident that in the Psalms, "the Lord God is a sun"; that Jesus is referred to as the "Sun of Righteousness"; or that a well-known Christmas carol refers to him as "risen with healing in his wings." One common ancient depiction of the rising sun showed it with wings. All the earliest gods or heroes were sun gods, and the halos shown behind saintly figures in early art derived originally from solar imagery. It was everywhere in ancient religion. A third-century painting in a crypt under the Vatican depicts Christ in a winged sun chariot as a solar god.

Had a Christian mob not destroyed one of the most treasured libraries of all time, that of the Druids at Bibracte in what was then Gaul in the early centuries of church history, we would know more of all of this, including the profound solar-cycle meaning behind the great stones of Salisbury Plain, the still-mysterious, brooding Stonehenge. But ever since the discovery and deciphering of the Rosetta stone about two hundred years ago, the sun-based religion of ancient Egypt has been unfolded by many scholars. It obviously greatly influenced both Judaism and Christianity.

The coming autumn equinox was for the world's earliest theologians the point at which the sun began to grow older and weaker in its battle against the forces of darkness. The god was about to "die" only to be reborn at or just three days after the shortest day of the year, the winter solstice. That's why December 25 became the birthday of all the gods, from Mithras to the Christ.

Significantly, on ancient Egyptian pyramid walls, Horus, the Egyptian Christ, was depicted either as a radiant, vigorous young man (the sun in the first six months of the year or at its height daily in the heavens), or as a decrepit, ugly old man (the sun in its declining months or in the evening). Hence the expressions "Double Horus" or "Horus of the Two Horizons." The same was true in early Christian art as well; Christ was represented as either one or the other, youthful and vigorous or old and ugly. The underlying symbolism was solar in origin.

For an early Jewish parallel adopted by the Christians but based originally on the Egyptian sources, reread Isaiah 53. It says in part— describing God's anointed servant or the Christ, a word which means anointed: "He hath no form nor comeliness; and when we see him there is no beauty that we should desire him. He is despised and rejected. . . ." This is fully based on the solar analogy.

The inner eternal meaning which all of this natural symbolism was intended to embed was a complex, many-splendoured thing. None of the great thinkers behind it all believed that the sun was literally God. However, they knew of no more powerful or abiding way to speak of the wisdom essential for human self-understanding and progress towards the ultimate evolutionary goal.

Not only was the dying sun a symbol of the divine willingness to sacrifice himself/itself on our behalf, it was also a supremely esoteric or hidden way of depicting the great theme of Incarnation. The sun's "sinking"—daily in the west as well as annually—was a symbol of God's pouring out of God's own nature in "seed" or "spark" form to every human born. The daily morning sunrise spoke of final, glorious Resurrection.

In the autumn, then, Spirit, in other words, was descending into matter. Matter, in turn (the word's origins mean mother), then gives birth to Spirit, symbolized at Christmas. As it is nurtured, the soul or spirit in every person is destined for "Christhood" on its own coming Easter Day. There is more going on here than meets the eye. The approaching fall, the equinox, the "death" of winter, the spring equinox and the joy of coming spring have depths to meet the spirit, heart and mind as well.

HALLOWEEN REMINDER OF
SPIRITUAL HARVEST TO COME

Few people today realize that when the children come knocking at their doors on Halloween dressed up in costumes and disguises of every sort, they are actually taking part in the remnants of a ritual with profound meaning dating back to primitive times.

It's no accident that Halloween occurs forty days following the September 21 equinox. As the sun moves across that autumnal line and the days begin to shorten, this symbolizes the soul's descent to birth or Incarnation on the human plane of Earth. The number forty, which occurs some sixty-four times in the Bible, is steeped in meaning. It represents a cardinal time of gestation or of incubation—for example, the normal cycle from conception to the birth of a baby is forty weeks.

The masks and robes were originally always the hides or replicas of various animals. The festival being celebrated was one of four great annual rites almost universally marked in the ancient world up to and overlapping with the emergence and eventual triumph of Christianity. Of these today only Christmas and Easter retain their proper splendour. It is being left to the followers of what is called a growing neo-paganism to observe in fullness both the autumn equinox and the summer solstice, the great "festival of fire."

Thus, Halloween is the celebration of our animal-divine nature, our full humanity. True, traditionally there have also been some clownish dimensions to the festivities in acknowledgment that when the soul enters the world of sense, it often behaves in foolish ways. (The first card of the tarot pack is the Fool.) Tomorrow, All Saints' Day, symbolizes the ultimate destiny for which we are intended: true fulfillment of the universal longing to be "made perfect," sanctified, fit for eternity and for God.

The equinox is the point at which the sun—a symbol of the divine soul in each of us—descends across the line, which, for ancient theology, marked the division between our disembodied spirit state and our enfleshment in matter.

The sun going down towards the winter solstice, or shortest day of the year, symbolized the descent into matter, that is, our taking on bodily existence. In other words, the huge spiritual truth that we are all sparks of the divine, incarnate in animal bodies, was being boldly depicted in nature's drama.

Wearing skins and animal masks signified this deep truth. The clowning, pranks and other shenanigans sometimes marking this night are echoes of the belief that the newly embodied souls had real difficulty adjusting to the very new experience of being set loose, as it were, to cope with the life of sense and emotion through which their earthly experience was to be garnered.

It's truly extraordinary when you begin to notice just how universally this theme of animals depicting humans runs throughout world literature, from the oldest fairy tales and folkloric sagas to the most elevated epics and novels. Studies of native peoples of our West Coast, or indeed of aboriginal peoples everywhere, reveal every possible variation upon this same theme of animal masks and antics for profoundly religious purposes. Behind it all lies this same reality, however much at times distorted, often with its original meaning forgotten.

In his 1956 classic study *The Hero*, written some years before Joseph Campbell's better-known treatise on the same theme, Lord Raglan writes: "A prominent feature of every type of traditional narrative (i.e. fictional tale) is the human being in animal form, or, what is . . . merely a variant, the animal that talks." Raglan goes on to say that the truth that persons disguised as animals are an almost universal feature of ancient ritual and drama is so well attested as to hardly need demonstration.

Whether you're religious or not, you probably don't know there is a talking donkey in the Bible. This apparent oddity is found in the Book of Numbers and is one more proof—if any were needed—that the bulk of the Bible is made up of allegorical and mythical truths. If anything is typical of traditional epics, sagas and folk tales, it is the presence in the text of animals that can speak.

The story in Numbers 22 tells how the prophet Balaam set out on a donkey to make a journey God had forbidden him to undertake. On the way, "the angel of the Lord" blocked his way with a drawn sword. Yet he was "seen" only by the ass. She balked and the prophet then "smote" her to force her to proceed.

The same thing happened a second time at a narrow place, and in trying to avoid the angel, the donkey "thrust herself into the wall," thus crushing Balaam's foot. Enraged, he beat her and forced her to go on. The third time (three plays a key role in all ancient traditional tales) the spot was too narrow for any evasion and so the donkey "fell down under Balaam" and he again "smote the ass with a staff."

At that, the donkey speaks and asks what she has done to merit such punishment. Her master replies that she has mocked him thrice and that if he had a sword he would kill her instantly. Then the beast points out her years of faithful service and "the Lord opened the eyes of Balaam" so that he saw the Angel of Death and learned how the animal had saved his life.

Such talking animals, whether in the Bible, primitive religious rituals, epic poetry or fairy tales, are always a reminder of a fundamental aspect of human evolution and of our overall, complex constitutions as human beings. Halloween, "the holy evening," is also a powerful reminder of the same salient truth. To quote Plato, one of the greatest masters of soul science the world has ever known, "we are gods as to intellect but in body we are animals."

To ask why children wear masks, particularly animal masks, on Halloween is essentially the same as asking why the initiates of the religion of Mithras wore animal skins in various initiation rites;

why ancient Egyptian gods had the bodies of humans but the heads of an extraordinary range of animals and birds; why the Hindu god Ganesh has an elephant's head; or why the Christ is often symbolized by a lamb.

Alvin Boyd Kuhn, in his remarkable 1940 book *The Lost Light*, tells how the Incarnation of God's spirit into us was "incontestably the most fateful event that had ever taken place in the evolutionary career of animal-man, giving him a status far above that of his former condition."

Countless Bible stories, sometimes quite odd and even meaningless on their own or taken literally, positively radiate with new spiritual power once this basic truth is recognized: The central theme of all religion is Incarnation, the god-in-man reality.

Take the story of Daniel in the lion's den. This is not about a remote miracle long ago and far away. It speaks to our condition at this moment. Though we are caught in the confines and severe testing of the "fire" of earthly bonds, the "Christos" or divine spirit within is constantly preserved by the prevailing power of God. Our soul is preserved from animal instincts as it holds fast to the divine ideal or its "higher self."

The same is true of Jonah in the belly of the great fish or of the story in the Book of Daniel in which King Nebuchadnezzar was given "the mind of an animal and his dwelling was with the wild beasts." The king here stands for the god within, and after his period of animality—eating grass like a wild beast—he is restored and cries, "My reason returned to me." In other words, once the period of our Incarnation is completed, a glorious future awaits.

For the ancients of Plato's time, and even long before in Egypt and elsewhere, the knowledge that we are spiritual beings or "souls" incarnated—enfleshed—in animal bodies was the basic datum of all reflection about who we really are and where we are really going. You see this in the thousands of stories from around the world of animals who are suddenly transformed into shining princes or beautiful princesses by a kiss, a magic wand or the slaying of some monstrous dragon. These are a coded way of witnessing to the truth that, within all our animal natures lies the potential to realize true divinization or "the Christ within."

In our own Incarnation, the divine seed has been planted within. Halloween reminds us of this and of a future, spiritual harvest to come.

SAINTS EXIST IN
EVERY RELIGION ON EARTH

For more than a thousand years, the now nearly two billion Christians of the globe have celebrated two major festivals on the first two days of November. November 1 is All Saints' Day. November 2 is normally the date of All Souls' Day, but whenever it falls on a Sunday it is moved ahead to November 3.

You may well be asking, "So what?"

Well, a lot is at stake for everybody once you realize the deeper meanings behind those festivals. All Saints' Day is appointed for remembering all Christian saints, known and unknown, who have been heroes of service to God and humanity from the beginning of time. Narrow church dogma, I know, would try to restrict this term to purely sectarian explanations dealing with "our people," "our communities," "our traditions," or even to those select persons technically canonized by churchy rules and rites—as has been recently happening in Rome.

Human understanding, however, has moved far ahead of doctrinaire exclusivity. In any case, let's deal with the latter part first, that saints refers only to those duly canonized by the Vatican or other hierarchies. The New Testament makes it plain on almost every page that each single member of the ekklesia, the body of the Christ, is considered a saint. In his writings Paul constantly refers to every member of the early churches as "called to be saints," that is, holy in the sense of being whole people dedicated to the service, care and encouragement of one another and to the larger human family. There were to be no exclusive elites in spite of some achieving heroic stature.

But, as hinted previously, there are saints in every religion on Earth. What's more, in my travels I have met atheist and agnostic saints, people wholly dedicated, under sometimes appalling circumstances, to the relief of human suffering and need. Who would dare not to reverence and respect their self-giving and utter singleness of heart regardless of their possession or lack of "proper" religious credentials? Certainly God, whom the Bible says is "no respecter of persons," would never draw the sanitized distinctions so glibly at hand for the self-righteous judges in our midst.

So, All Saints' was and is an important day, a moment to think with gratitude not of the celebrities of public charity—the winners of the Order of Canada or the Nobel Peace Prize—but of those unseen, unknown thousands, yes, millions of people next door or down the street, or in dark hospices for AIDS patients in African villages, in hospitals in Calcutta or on the streets of Nairobi, who tend to the sick and dying, who feed the hungry, who befriend the homeless, who listen to the lonely, who in their own quiet way fight for justice every waking hour. These are the unsung folk who make a more humane and human life possible for everyone. They're forwarding the evolutionary thrust—though but a fraction—every day.

What of this year's All Souls' Day? That is the great festival of affirmation of the truth that death is indeed "swallowed up in victory." On that day, the church reminds the whole of humanity of a truth far larger than the institution itself can ever, or indeed will ever, be. Though traditionally the church came to restrict its belief in a fuller dimension of life, a glory beyond compare, after death to only "the faithful"—to those considered by the proper authorities to have died holding the approved credentials (what a power trip!), this was not so at its beginnings.

Such brilliant theologians as Origen of Alexandria (185–254 C.E.) believed that ultimately what the name actually says—All Souls—would enter and inherit the "life of the age to come." We call this view Universalism and it is certainly one I share with many true Christians today. Origen was later declared a heretic for this belief among others, and not only were his books banned or burned, anyone who dared to read them was excommunicated (damned).

When I'm able to be in Toronto on All Souls' Day, I slip into the silence of St. James Cathedral and light some candles. There would be one for each of our parents, one for Sue's brother, Ivan, and one for all souls everywhere who have gone on before. They are all around us. The flames symbolize our never-failing "reasonable hope" of this reality.

MILITARY PRAYER HAS DARK SIDE

My earliest Remembrance Day memories are of standing near my school in the east end of Toronto on a crisp November 11 morning, keenly aware of butterflies within and the cold bite of a bugle's brass coil in my hand. I was awaiting the cue for playing the last post and then reveille. They were moments of high anxiety because a bugle's notes are certain to be unforgiving if wrongly sounded. I had practised long, however, and can say without immodesty, had become at a tender age the leading bugler in our neighbourhood. (Yes, I know, blowing my own horn.)

Over the intervening span of time, my thoughts and feelings about this day have matured and deepened. It has come to mean much more than it ever did before. We plan to be in the town's core whatever the weather on Remembrance Day this year as our community, like Toronto, Ottawa and thousands of places of all sizes across the land, solemnly remembers the death of its youth on far-flung battlefields.

As the tableau unfolds of bands and marching, the ever-shrinking knot of veterans proudly passing by, the laying of wreaths and the prayers, the sharp commands ringing out and echoing from the walls of the town hall and nearby shops as the colour-guard salutes the dead, my emotions will be once again those of rising anger more than grief. Grief, certainly, and gratitude, but increasingly there's anger at the folly and monumental hypocrisy of our so-called civilization over the ungodly horror known as war. The technology for slaughter has made demonic advances light-years ahead of our moral evolution as bearers of the name *Homo sapiens*.

Has anything changed since we played this drama last year, or the year before, or since we turned into this new millennium? Are the nations of the world any less eager to rush into battle than a decade ago, a generation, even a century? And how can the churches and the rest of the world's religions still give their blessings, sprinkle their holy water, and pray each for their own side to win? The United States now basking in the role of the world's lone super-power and claiming to be God's chosen vessel for global hegemony is mired in war and readying itself for deadlier confrontations. The globe's "most Christian country" has the backing of the majority of its Christian constituency on every front. The line between church and state gets blurred beyond recognition.

Why are there not more prophetic voices being heard? We have to turn to one long dead who yet still speaks. I refer to one of America's best-known sons, a man who though not religious at all never-theless spoke out against religion's blessing of arms as policy more forcefully than anybody since. That man was Mark Twain.

In 1904, during the Philippine–American War, Twain wrote *The War Prayer*, but it was never published until found amongst his papers after his death. In the preamble, he described a time not unlike the current climate in the U.S. The country was up in arms, patriotism and jingoistic slogans were in the air and in the churches as pastors preached devotion to flag and nation "and invoked the God of Battles" against the devilish enemy. Rash spirits who dared disapprove of the war and cast doubts on its righteousness received such angry rebukes they quickly shrank away, fearing for their safety.

Twain then describes a typical service on the eve of soldiers leaving for the war zone, the hymns, the glowing words, the envy of those who had no sons to send to glory. Then came a long prayer—none could remember the like of it for passion and pleading. God was entreated to watch over their troops and protect them in their patriotic duties . . . "help them to crush the foe and grant to them, their flag and country, imperishable honour. . . ."

Suddenly, an aged stranger with burning eyes enters and, motioning the minister aside, announces he has come from the "Throne of God" with a message. It is the hidden, other half of the eloquent prayer for victory the minister has just pronounced. It is its necessary concomitant, so God declares. A few lines give Twain's satirical intent:

> O Lord . . . help us to tear their soldiers to bloody shreds with our shells; help us to cover their . . . fields with the pale forms of their patriotic dead; help us to drown the thunder of the guns with the shrieks of their wounded, writhing in pain; help us to lay waste their humble homes with a hurricane of fire. . . .

It goes on in mounting, terrible words to describe all the hellish nightmares that attend war, and ends: "We ask it in the spirit of love, of Him who is the source of love . . . Amen."

Twain made no claims to piety. But I find his words still ringing with more power than any sermon on war that I have ever heard.

WINTER

WINTER'S SPIRITUAL BLESSINGS

We had just returned from some time in the southern U.S.—part holiday, part research. Though we saw the aftermath of two savage tornadoes in Georgia, the weather as we drove north was sunny. Roads and fields were bare all the way to the Canadian border.

In Ontario, a dramatic change occurred. We were plunged into full winter. Since our home is out in the country, we stopped near Windsor and phoned to make sure our long lane had been ploughed and a path cleared to the door. We also changed clothes, digging out the long underwear once more.

On arrival, we managed to get up the lane, between the snow-banks. But unloading often meant having to step off into drifts at least a metre deep. Our 1890-built farmhouse sits high on a hillside overlooking a lake in one direction and a valley in another. The snow loves the house, swathing it and every tree, bush and lawn thickly with a fresh layer of wrapping at every chance.

Lighting the airtight stove, fetching more kindling from outside and doing myriad other chores as the radio blared warnings of a fresh storm—the "storm of the winter"—you had to wonder why we of the northern hemisphere all choose to live in such a bleak deep-freeze!

In spite of the obvious "dark side" of winter—the colds and flu, the weight of clothing, the greyness at times and the piercing frost, the short days and the hardships of just getting around—many of us have a deep love for all the gifts that only winter can bring. Personally, I now believe that winter is the most spiritual season of all.

There was a huge full moon in the east when we looked out from the top-floor window before bed that night. It lit up the landscape for miles around as the snow shone like an endless reflector. The holy stillness and the magical beauty kindled deep feelings of awe.

The days of near-blinding sunshine that followed have turned a world of icicles, drifts and silence into a spectacle of miracles—a feast for the senses and for the heart. Even the humblest twigs or the ugliest weeds are now brilliant with frost diamonds and bask in glory.

Beauty is one of the most profoundly spiritual experiences we can have and by becoming more sensitive to it, especially in seemingly unlikely places, our inner life is steadily quickened and fed. For example, few things are lovelier than a stream covered by ice and snow yet somehow breaking through here and there with joyous gurgling and a sparkling flow. One seems to hear a cosmic chuckle, a divine laughter from the heart of the Earth, a promise of spring.

I have grown to love the look of bare branches against the winter sky and to see the way—with all the leaves stripped and shorn—the hills and valleys stand out starkly in their nakedness. The skeleton of the entire landscape lies boldly exposed. One can draw on its sheer strength and honesty for one's soul's growth.

Winter is a time when all of life appears to have been put on hold, a time when we can reflect on what has been and on what may be ahead. If we're fully aware, the vital moment we call "now" can be stretched a little. We can focus more on being rather than on doing or making. We can learn much from the patience and the silent waiting of all nature. Significantly, the Hebrew Bible and so many other scriptures stress the importance for each of us to "wait upon God" if spiritual progress is to be made.

More and more from winter I am learning the truth of what great spiritual teachers have always taught: It is important to pursue right actions. But it is even more important sometimes not to act at all. Winter is an ideal time for quiet and contemplation; for simply sitting still.

Winter is not about laziness, of course. The "waiting" is a pregnant one. As the American poet John Greenleaf Whittier once wrote:

The Night is mother of the Day,
The Winter of the Spring.

You can look out at a wintry scene and feel depressed or forlorn. Nature can seem analogous to death. But have you ever considered just how incredible is the power and energy lying latent all around us at that time of year? In a few weeks, the icy grip will gradually relax and Earth will burst forth with such a tremendous surge that no technology can begin to gauge its massive renewing power. As I write, this infinite potentiality is preparing to transform our world. Similarly, this same kind of hidden potency sleeps yet within our inmost selves as well. Every great spiritual tradition affirms that "all things are possible with God."

Long ago, in my final year at the University of Toronto, I was walking up past the Royal Ontario Museum in early December. It was growing dark, a raw, damp evening. Winter loomed. My mood had been strangely blue for a couple of days. Suddenly, a small maple on the sidewalk's edge practically ordered me to examine it. I did and to my amazement I saw that in spite of the cold, it was already covered with buds. I suddenly felt a great lifting within. "The vision splendid" had transfigured my soul.

CHRISTMAS

And the light shines on in the darkness; and the darkness has not overwhelmed it . . . That was the essence of light itself, the same light that imparts light to every person who comes into the world.

— From the Prologue to John's Gospel;
my translation of the Greek text

———————

At the time decided by the early Christians to be the birth of Christ, there was a unique Jewish sect living at Qumran, overlooking the bitter waters of the Dead Sea on one side and the arid hills of the Judean wilderness on the other. Ever since the discovery of the Dead Sea scrolls in caves near the ruins of Qumran in 1947, we have known that these ascetics had fled what they saw as the worldliness of Jerusalem. They were waiting for the end time, when the ultimate struggle between the forces of light and darkness would take place and usher in the Messianic Age.

In using the imagery of light and darkness, they were picking up mythical symbolism that came from Persia—from the Zoroastrians who worshipped Ahura Mazda, God of Light, whose sacred symbol was and still is fire. (Incidentally, it is likely that the Magi were in fact Zoroastrian astrologers or priests.) But students of religion and mythology know that the deep, human perception that God is "the essence of light" and that there is a cosmic struggle always going on between good (light) and evil (darkness) has roots that are universal and as old as humanity itself. Speaking of Brahman, "the Lord God," the Upanishads or Hindu scriptures, written hundreds of years before the birth of Christ, say: "Thou alone art—thou the Light Imperishable . . ."

The same awareness lies behind primitive worship of the sun. In fact, it was inevitable that when the early Christians wanted to set a day to mark the birth of Jesus they chose a day already long in use by the Romans to mark the Dies Natalis, or birthday of the sun. As the shortest day of the year approached, the winter solstice, it was no wonder pagan peoples felt there was a risk the sun might die or be extinguished altogether. By lighting fires, torches and candles, they encouraged its rekindling and then feasted to celebrate the renewal of the cosmic cycle once again. At this season, when Jews light candles for the festival of Chanukah or when Christians—active or lapsed—display Christmas lights and gather for festive meals, there are echoes of this vast, primeval drama.

We miss the point, however, if we fail to go beyond the various outward trappings and symbols surrounding any religious occasion, to the inner or spiritual meaning.

The quote with which I began says that the Christ Event is a supreme example of the divine Light coming into this world, a light that is the very source of the light or presence of God in every human being. What's more, it states that, however daunting and oppressive the darkness, it has never (and can never) wholly overcome the light or goodness of God.

We need to hear this. We need to because it's so easy at times to look at the world around us and feel that the darkness is about to engulf us. We read or hear and see the news and are sorely tempted to believe that evil has the upper hand, that injustice, inhumanity and war are about to eclipse all vestiges of light. The spiritual meaning of Christmas is that this does not have to be the case. The light has never been put out. Always throughout history, even at the darkest hour, here or there—often in the most unexpected, least esteemed places—there have been flickers of light.

You see, as John's Gospel says, each one of us is a light-bearer. The essence of light itself, God, has kindled the flame in us. It is the individuals who keep the faith with that inner light who make the difference in this world. Whenever a cup of cold water is given to the thirsty, whenever compassion of any kind is shown or the burden lifted from the shoulders of the weak and helpless, whenever depravity is resisted or the oppressor is rebuked, whenever justice is defended or the sick in body and mind are healed, and the lonely comforted, whenever truth is spoken or done, there is light—and God is there.

Challenging as it may seem, we are all of us called to be the light of the world as the divine Light itself channels through us. As the Hindu scripture also says: "The Atman [God within] is the light. The light is covered by darkness . . . but when the light of the Atman drives out our darkness, that light shines forth from us and God is revealed."

Darkness still stalks the Earth as it did that first Christmas long ago. There is torture and poverty, there is violence against women and children, there is hunger and unemployment. But the darkness has not overwhelmed the light—nor will it ever. The heart of Christmas is not some sentimental or nostalgic orgy of feelings. It's not about eating, drinking and getting gifts. It's about letting that light be born afresh in the manger of your soul and taking arms anew in the fight against the dark.

WE ARE ALL CHILDREN
OF THE ELEMENTAL FIRE

We only live, only suspire / Consumed by either fire or fire.
— T. S. ELIOT, *The Four Quartets*

The Lord is my light—Dominus Illuminatio Mea
— Oxford University motto, from PSALM 27:1

Christmas is supremely a festival of fire and of light. The symbolism is everywhere: the candles, the Yule log, the tree decorations, the coloured lights on all sides, the fact that December 25 comes just after the winter solstice, the rebirth of the sun. All religions have festivals of light at one point or another in their calendar. December 25 was the birthday of all the ancient sun gods, especially Mithras, the archrival of the early Christian movement who was born in a cave.

God is a consuming fire, the Bible says. But it means this metaphorically, as Eliot also does in the opening quote. God is the fire of love. There is either the fire of ego or the fire of love. Life is about burning with one or the other—at times, painfully, with both at the same time. That is when our "eye" is no longer single; our "house" is divided, in danger of falling in on us.

Looked at another way, we are all children of the elemental fire. We come from the nuclear fires of the sun, that ancient cosmic symbol of divine Mind and hence of the eternal Logos, the Christ. The Logos, God's self-manifestation in all creation, every galaxy, every star, every plant, every creature, was the "true light that imparts light to every person coming into the world."

According to the scientists at the Sudbury Neutrino Observatory, buried two kilometres deep in a mine shaft to avoid radioactive "interference," the Earth and everything on it, including us, are continuously being penetrated by sunlight. Every one of the many billions of cells in your body at this moment contains infinitesimally tiny units of solar energy. Billions of neutrinos are passing through my fingers as I type.

As the old Hindu mantra which I often use in my own prayers puts it: "We are created by the divine Light; we are sustained by the divine Light; we are protected by the divine Light; we are surrounded by the divine Light; we are filled by the divine Light; we are daily growing into the divine Light."

The Gospel Christ says he is the light of the world; but he also says to us: "You are the light of the world." The levels of meaning here are many-splendoured, richly glowing.

Behind all significance given to candles in the various world's religions, there's one esoteric or inner symbol of great transformative power. Some time over this Christmas season, get by yourself. Look at a burning candle quietly and attentively. Be still. What you are watching is a living parable of your life and of mine and that of every other human being alive today. The flame represents the spirit bestowed by the Creator upon everyone created in his/her image. Recognized, or, to change the metaphor, birthed and nourished for what it is, this symbolizes the divine presence, the Christ within. Other faiths have different names. The reality, however, remains the same.

Notice the flame is at the "head" of the candle—as mind/spirit is always associated with the head and brain. (Anointing the head with oil, one of Earth's most ancient religious symbolisms, signified the divine gift of the "fire" of mind-power. Oil, being flammable, was used universally for this reason.) As the candle burns, the tallow (signifying our animal aspect) miraculously is metamorphosed into something different—warmth, spreading light, a spirit-like mix. This mirrors allegorically the way the soul's tenancy of the body was thought of by ancient sages as gradually drawing up our lower elements and transmuting them into its own glorious essence of spirit/fire. This is what was meant of old by "the Purification of the Virgin."

The second of February, a symbolic forty days after Christmas (it took forty days for a seed to mature, forty weeks for a fetus to develop), is known in the church as Candlemas Day, or the day of the Purification of the Virgin. It's a time for the blessing of candles.

All of this is why St. Thomas Aquinas once quoted St. Clement of Alexandria (c.150–215) from centuries before and wrote: "The candle is the sign of the Christ. . . ."

GOD IS WITH US,
FOR US AND IN US

Sitting by the fire at Christmastide, many of us are visited by the ghosts of Christmases past.

Every December for many years when I was religion editor, the *Star* unleashed a photographer and me to roam the globe in search of inspirational stories. They were tales of hope and ran each year as front-page specials for several days at a time leading up to December 25. Those explorations left an indelible imprint on my mind and soul and the images they conjure up in the firelight now are as vivid as they first were some twenty years ago.

What these opportunities taught has been distilled with the passing years into a kind of simple wisdom for the soul. It's a deposit out of which those many who are hurting at this festive season of the year hopefully may find some comfort. I call my discovery "The Grammar of God." But first allow me to reminisce a little:

In 1976, the *Star* sent photographer Dick Loek and me to Israel. The series was called "The Road to Bethlehem 2000 Years Later." We rented a donkey in Nazareth in the hilly north and walked the 165 kilometres from there down the Jordan Valley to Jericho, up the steepish climb to Jerusalem, and then on to Bethlehem. The trip took five days and was wholly unforgettable. You get to know a country when you walk it like that. The wilderness was particularly impressive.

In 1977, we went to Frobisher Bay, Pangnirtung, Broughton Island and other parts of Baffin Island in the eastern Arctic. We hunted seals (didn't see any) with an Inuit Anglican priest out on the polar ice facing Greenland and spent a night in an igloo. It was like trying to sleep in a freezer at the supermarket. The people were wonderful and the landscape hauntingly beautiful in the half-light of Arctic winter.

The next year found us looking for "signs of hope" in Europe for a series by that title. We spent time in Kraków, Poland, where rejoicing over the recent election of Cardinal Karol Wojtyla to be the first non-Italian pope in well over four hundred years still had his compatriots in a frenzy. From there we went to a thriving orphanage (Protestant, surprisingly) in the teeming outskirts of Naples— Casa Materna—then to l'Arche, in France, to visit with Jean Vanier and see his compassionate ministry to severely challenged young men there; then on to the remote, windswept island of Iona, off the rugged western coast of Scotland, where Sir George McCleod had restored the ancient site and re-established a missionary centre to bring good news to urbanized Britain.

The 1979 series was called "Christmas in Asia." Photographer Bob Olsen and I spent a week in Calcutta watching Mother Teresa at work in her orphanage and in the House of the Dying. We also spent time with the too little praised, late Reverend Mark Buntain, "St. Mark of Calcutta," who, with his wife, Huldah, was working miracles by training street children for meaningful careers, feeding the hungry and running one of the most modern hospitals (which he built) in India. Buntain, a Pentecostal, was Canadian-born and his claim to fame has been eclipsed by his saintly peer.

We went next to Kathmandu, Nepal, and from there, on foot, across endless rice paddies and by rope bridges over breathtaking gorges into the foothills of the Himalayas. There, at Amp Pipal, a mountainside jungle village, we met Canadian doctor Helen Huston, of the United Church, a physician "on the roof of the world."

In 1980, back to Israel and on to Egypt for a series entitled "A Tale of Two Mountains." We slept out at the hill near the Sea of Galilee where tradition says the Sermon on the Mount was given, and later climbed and camped on top of Mount Sinai above the ancient monastery of St. Catherines. It was a "moonscape" near the Red Sea.

There's so much more, but space runs out. What did I learn? What have all these "ghosts" to say? In The Grammar of God, three prepositions stand out for me through it all. God is with us. That's what Emmanuel means: God with us. That's what Christmas means: God with us—always. We don't need to sing "O come, O come, Emmanuel." The reality is here already. Then, too, God is for us. As St. Paul says: "If God be for us, who—or what—can be against us?" Fantastic!

Most important, God is in us. Christmas is about Incarnation, that is, about God being "born" in us. It's the most important truth I've ever learned. God is in us all.

THE CHRISTMAS MYTH IS
THE STORY OF HUMAN FAMILY

———————————

At this year's Christmas, as the familiar patterns unroll themselves once again—the music, the tinsel, the stress of shopping, the crowded supermarkets with their glut of food, the parties, the strain of forced family togetherness when often the chemistry isn't there, the religious rituals with their words of peace in a world that knows no peace, the joys, some real some feigned, the griefs of those somehow left out—will there be any difference from a year, two years, ten years ago?

Will we have come any closer, in spite of the Nativity scenes, the carols, the masses, the sermons or the "smells and bells" of packed churches, any closer to the real meaning beneath it all? Or will it be yet one more telling of a simplistic tale that is charming in its rusticity, quaint in all its various "props," yet utterly remote from one's deepest fears, longings and hopes, remote from the grit and pulse of life as we and every other sojourner on Earth must live it daily?

A vast segment of humanity has been telling itself this same story of a baby born in a manger in Bethlehem for many centuries now; peace and goodwill towards all the clan of *Homo sapiens*. But nothing has changed. Bethlehem itself has become synonymous with violence. Just now, as the Christmas fervour is being driven towards its annual climax, once-Christian nations are waging war against other countries.

What is the deeper story that has somehow been twisted wholly out of shape and so layered over with trite or fraudulent wrappings that the real gift is rarely ever envisioned let alone observed and gratefully received? Is there, was there ever some precious thing of matchless beauty, power and grace at the very heart of Christmas—something with flaming potency to transform our lives, our world?

The answer is a resounding, all-embracing yes, but it's not won by glib or lazy wishful thinking. Mere repetition of literalistic tales and pious traditions can never get us there. One can go through the entire process by rote or on automatic pilot, and miss the "many-splendoured thing."

This brings us to what many may find to be a tough medicine or even drastic surgery. But if one is to pass beyond the childish and the external to the core of what Christmas is all about, it's an essential step. What one has to realize first of all is that the story of the birth of Jesus is a myth. No, not a fairy tale, not a legend, not a piece of fiction to be seen through and dropped at puberty or before, but a spiritual myth—in other words, a truth so vast and so important to our human condition that it can only be told in the most profound language of all, the language of symbolism, allegory and metaphor.

As the late authority on myth, Joseph Campbell, repeated time and again, myth is infinitely more transformative and true than history any time. This cannot be stressed enough. We use myth as synonymous with that which is untrue when ironically its fundamental meaning in all the deepest wisdoms known is the total opposite. What is historical is fleeting, open to a hundred viewpoints—for example, who really killed JFK and why? But the meaning of the myth is always eternal.

The truth is that the myth told at Christmas is the oldest myth known to us. The birth of a divine King's son, into humble circumstances, amidst threats to his life, accompanied by angelic greetings, rejoicing shepherds, and visited by three Magi while a spectacular star shines overhead, is almost as old as humanity. It was known in ancient Sumeria and Egypt many thousands of years B.C.E. It belongs to every religion and clime. It's an eternal story.

This is a mythos that links every one of us to the Ground of our being—to God or the Ultimate—but also to Earth and the solar system, to all of nature, and thus to one another. What it's about is the evolutionary "moment" in human development when Spirit entered into the animal kingdom and "became man," that is, a humanoid capable of self-reflective intelligence and so of moral choices. That's the point of "born in a manger" in a stable surrounded by beasts. The divine enters the animal at a place where, symbolically, animals "eat" (French *manger*) and God's Logos or Word finally becomes "flesh."

Christmas came to be celebrated on December 25 (birthday of all ancient gods), three days after the winter solstice because in the myth, the rebirth of the sun on the twenty-first symbolized this fact of Incarnation (*in* + *carnem* = in the flesh) better than any other cosmic reality.

The mythos of a Virgin Birth is also a common motif of the past. Dozens of examples from that period can be cited. What is really being said by it has nothing to do with contradicting natural biology. Rather, the meaning lies in the truth that whatever else this birth is, it is God's act. It says that Jesus was being sent as the pre-eminent Agent and Word of God. The Virgin Birth was not known to Paul, Mark or the author of John's Gospel. It was clearly not part of the earliest preaching in Acts.

The Christmas mythos tells us that Jesus was born of God and that ultimately we all are too. Unlike him, however, the majority of us have not yet consciously had this Virgin Birth, or awakening in our souls as to what or who we have been created to be. In the birth of every baby, the Word is "made flesh." That's the ultimate meaning of Christmas.

The Christmas myth is your story, and that of your partner or child, your sibling or parent, your neighbour, and the people of Iraq and other nations experiencing turmoil. It's the story of our human family. God dwells in every heart. The joy of Christmas means awakening to this fact.

A NEW LAYER TO CHRISTMAS

Every year one hears how we should remember "the meaning of Christmas"—often with a vague sense of guilt. The problem lies in supposing that there is only one meaning to be either found or ignored. Nothing could be less true. Christmas is multidimensional, holding many layers of meaning. At some levels, it speaks of realities so vast, yet so simple, that it has universal appeal. Whether you are an atheist, a secular spiritual seeker or a believer in any one of the various religions now in our midst, this Christmas is for you.

There are two important ways in which this can be illustrated (apart from lesser aspects—such as the commercialism which is deplored by most yet eventually benefits all). The first is the cosmic connection; the second is the light beyond all light.

First, think of the cosmic connection. There's a deeply spiritual chord here that resonates with the essence of every creature and organism on our planet. It stems from the way Christmas marks the all-embracing solar cycles and the "return" of the sun. On and around December 21, the shortest day of the year (the winter solstice—or "standing still of the sun"), earthlings have life itself at stake.

The ancient Romans, together with every tribe and culture on Earth at that time, marked the event with several days of feasting and lighting of fires. Indeed, lights of all kinds and sizes were displayed to encourage the sun god to grow in strength again. The early Christians simply "baptized" all of this and took it over. The birth of Christ was made to fit with the yearly rebirth of the great physical light which, through divine fiat, made possible and still sustains all things.

But besides reminding us of our deep involvement in the basic rhythms of the universe and hence of our spiritual stake in the global environment, Christmas bespeaks a very different kind of light or illumination altogether. Interestingly and intentionally, every major faith has a festival or season entirely devoted to light. This time, it may involve the sun but only as an image or sign of deeper reality. The actual "light" being spoken of is the Light of the divine Presence; it's the effulgence or shining forth of God.

The world over, the ubiquitous metaphor for God, the most potent and accessible picture to hold in mind when people think about or pray to God, is a light beyond all light. Thus, when the Psalmist says, "The Lord is my light and my salvation," or the prophet Isaiah writes, "Arise, shine, for your light has come and the glory of the Lord has risen upon you . . . ," they are voicing a profound insight. The Source of all things is wrapped and bathed in "light inaccessible, hid from our eyes," as the hymn writer says. He goes on: "It's only the splendour of light hideth thee."

Read as widely as you want in all the spiritual literature ever collected—from the Vedas to Paul's letters—and you will find that inner release, nirvana, heaven, spiritual bliss here and now, cosmic consciousness, every reference to peak religious experiences, all these and much more could and can only be expressed in terms of blazing, all-consuming, supernatural light.

Christmas, with its lights of every kind, tawdry as well as beautiful beyond compare, is meant for all because at its core or root is the ever-new conviction that the divine light behind, under and through all life does indeed break into our human consciousness and is the foundation of any hope we have for the future both here and hereafter. Other faiths witness the same.

There are four Gospels. One, Mark, which is the earliest, has nothing about the first Christmas. It begins not with Christ's infancy but with his baptism by John the Baptist. Matthew and Luke give us the Nativity Story as it developed. The accounts differ but also complement each other. For Matthew, the genealogy of

Jesus goes back to Abraham, to show him as a true Jew, fulfilling the promises. Luke traces a lineage going back to Adam, thus showing Jesus' relevance to all humanity.

But the Fourth Gospel, in many ways an enigma and certainly the latest, "most spiritual" of the four, tells the story quite uniquely—from a cosmic perspective. There is nothing about inns, mangers or wise men. Nothing about angelic choirs. In a conscious echo of Genesis, but taking, as it were, a view from space, "John" or his editor starts off: "In the beginning was the word (the primal creative sound or self-expression of God) . . ." He continues, in "prologue," by identifying Jesus with this "word" and the principle by which the world was made. With his birth or "coming into the world" true life entered, and this life "was the light of all people. The light shines in the darkness and the darkness did not overcome it. . . . The true light which enlightens everyone, was coming into the world."

Behind the canned carols, the wrapping paper and the commercial hype, recognize the divine Light within, God's gift to you. Whoever you are, Christian or not, don't miss this opportunity to give it room afresh in the manger of your soul.

TRANSFORMED INTO HEAT AND LIGHT

There is a book much more ancient than the Bible or any other sacred text.

This book is the very foundation of all other scriptures. It lies at the core of what I call a "cosmic spirituality." It is nature itself. Nature and the natural symbols drawn from it declare the mind of God more eloquently, more compellingly than all the wisdom ever channelled through the holiest of prophets, seers and saints. That's why, when many today are asking what the true or inner meaning of Christmas is, it is a mark of understanding to stop and look around, not at the cheap commercial tokenism or even the religious props abundant on every side, but at what the natural world is telling us.

It is not a coincidence that Christmas comes in the bleak midwinter, at that moment of deepest darkness when the days are shortest and we rush to warm our hands and feet by the nearest fire. Because of the yearly cycle of the stars, the sun and the planets, sages of old saw rightly that the winter solstice was the key turning point of all earthly life. Among many other things, it spoke to them of the near eclipse of the father of all lights, the solar source, and thus of the "night" of the soul's descent into dense matter—our human bodies.

All the ancient sun gods, Mithras, Dionysus and the rest had their birthdays—or rather "re-birthdays"—on December 25, three days after the nadir of the year was past. Thus it was inevitable, even though it took nearly four centuries before the church made it official, that the birth of Jesus would be celebrated on the same date.

The symbolism from nature of this annual triumph of light over darkness—"the light shone in the darkness and the darkness has never overcome it," as John says—may seem simple enough, but in "earthspeak" it is the simple things that are the most relevant and the most profound. No matter how foolishly, even insanely, we humans act towards one another or towards Earth itself, the light will ultimately shine as victor over all. That's not a pious guess. That's God's promise in his/her thoughts made manifest throughout creation.

One of the saddest things that has happened to Christianity because of its too-frequent scorn for the Book of Creation is that it has missed nature's central preoccupation, one might almost say obsession, with transformation here and now. Observe the world around you closely and you cannot escape this fundamental truth.

Take something as ordinary at this time of year—and as wonderful—as a blazing fire in the hearth. Few things are more expressive of the deep spiritual truth of transformation. As you watch meditatively, there's a reason for the spell of fascination that casts itself about you. The flickering flames throw light and heat as the wood is transformed from something dull and solid into dancing, airy, glowing energy. It's a parable of the way the "fire" of soul and spirit within us wants to mould and change us into beings of warmth and light.

The poet T. S. Eliot put it this way in *Little Gidding*: "We only live, only suspire, consumed by either fire or fire." What he meant was that one is either being transformed by the burning power of love or by the corrosion of selfishness and hate.

If you're one of those who wonder at this, the busiest and most hectic time of the year, "What's it about anyway? What meaning, if any, lies behind this mad scene?," find a fireplace somewhere and sit silently watching for a while. The changes you witness as you meditate can happen, spiritually speaking, in you.

Lacking a fireplace? Then find a candle, light it and sit still and see how the flame transforms the wax into something close to miraculous. Without a word being spoken, the entire message of Christmas is there. The story of Jesus is a parable of the birth of the soul's light within our own breast. This inner shining, by whatever name we call it, is to us what the candle's flame is to its solid base—the key to transformation.

You see, the problem with salvation, redemption or being "saved" is that the emphasis is upon the meaning of a presumed, historical Jesus as a saviour from outside, from another world. This takes the responsibility away from where it really rests—with us. We have had nearly two thousand years of allegedly external redemption. It's time for some genuine inner transformation instead.

As the medieval mystic Angelus Silesius once wrote: "God is the fire in me, I am the glow in Him." The world needs that awareness so badly. And the truly exciting thing is that it lies within the ready reach of every one of us.

4

PEARL OF
GREAT PRICE

*When he had found one pearl of great price he
went and sold all that he had and bought it.*

— MATTHEW 13:46

HUMAN NATURE ABHORS

INNER SPIRITUAL VACUUM

The spirituality of those who say they have no religion or who don't
consider themselves "religious" interests me greatly. Partly, the reason
is selfish. I identify closely with them in many ways. When the German martyr to Nazism, Dietrich Bonhoeffer, wrote that Jesus Christ
came to put an end to "religion," it was a thought that resonated
deeply within me even though I see the Christ quite differently now
than when I first read that comment years ago.

In a 2003 census, 16 percent of Canadians said that they considered themselves to be religionless. This was a staggering increase
over numbers from two decades ago, but it is of critical importance
to realize that it is far from meaning that we are fast becoming a
nation of atheists or agnostics.

The amount of spiritual and religious hunger today in our society
is deep, widespread, and not to be denied in its quest for satisfying

answers. While these "religionless" people may have given up on more traditional forms of belief and worship, most still believe in the surrounding, divine mystery we call God; they still pray in their own fashion; they continue to be fully committed to the Golden Rule in daily conduct; they're convinced that life has a deeper meaning than simply being born, getting a cellphone, a job, a car, a partner, and eventually retiring, before ending up in "sundown manor" and finally a grave.

But none of this should really surprise us. That such religionless people are nevertheless most often very spiritual or profoundly engaged in a spiritual journey of some kind is a necessary corollary of who we really are. Religions say we are all made in the image of God. Some believe there's a "hollow space" for this Presence inside every one of us. Our "souls are restless until they find their rest in Thee," as St. Augustine put it. Our nature abhors an inner vacuum.

Another way of stating it is to say that the human species can only be truly defined as a race of beings hard-wired for transcendence, for an experience of dimensions of being and consciousness far beyond the mundane or the purely sensual drives of our animal-based nature. We are essentially spiritual animals.

Regular readers of my columns know that the most ancient, inner wisdom of the great spiritual sages down the centuries—of all faiths and none—is that we all share in a spark of the divine fire. Our task is to recognize this inner gift, fan it into brighter flame, and let it shine on out for all the world to see and profit thereby.

It's my conviction that the so-called religionless millions of not just Canada but of the world today are coming in growing numbers to awaken to this "pearl of great price" within and are unconsciously growing together as they fathom its meaning for their lives. The potential for a different kind of world is enormous.

The steady decline of organized religion, in other words, may not be the terrible thing that many of the traditionally pious imagine. It's certainly not the kind of "turning to God" that many evangelists thunder on about. Yet it may well presage the beginning of a new and deeper spiritual awakening than any so-called "great revival" of the past.

WHAT'S "SPIRITUAL" AND WHAT'S NOT

———————

Every day my mail brings word of prestigious conferences and seminars on spirituality. The *S*-word has been well out of the closet for some time—and has even become a kind of cachet, a mark of assumed superiority or of being on the leading edge. For example, the medical world has begun to realize that patients are much more than mere thinking machines. Consequently, there are medical symposia on the spiritual needs of the sick, new courses at medical schools and many other clear signs of a changing model for "health." The business world too is increasingly aware of this new return to old knowledge, and has jumped on it as a cheap yet revolutionary approach to both staff and customers—a competitive advantage that is ethical as well as good for the bottom line.

There are great advantages and also dire risks in this pervasive development. In one way it's a sign that at a much deeper level something energizing and renewing is indeed going on. As many believe, there's a major groundswell of longing in our time for real soul nourishment instead of the secular slop presently served up by a culture whose chief characteristic tends to be its superficiality. But along with this unprecedented spiritual search—in motion in all the developed countries of the world—we also are finding that there are many who would warp or exploit it for their own ends. Hucksters and tricksters of all kinds abound.

People searching earnestly, sometimes desperately, for spiritual truth are frequently the most vulnerable to manipulation or outright deception. One of the things that surprises one most in this regard is the poor sense so many seekers have of what actually constitutes "evidence." I'm always amazed when the last thing many spiritual seekers seem interested in is the difference between fact and fancy, between a reasonable faith and blind belief. This only helps the predators.

In such a situation, we need some clear guidance—especially on how to discern false prophets from true ones and how to assess what's truly spiritual and what's not. Our religious and spiritual leaders could really connect to today's spiritual seekers if they spent some time thinking about what they believe are clear criteria for such a quest. A true dialogue could open.

Here are some guidelines from my experience to start the process. First, the negative:

- Avoid any doctrine, philosophy, rites or "secret knowledge" that must never be questioned or tested by a rational critique.

- Beware of offers of quick-fix, instant or magical spirituality. There's no easy path to inner growth or "soul-work." It can't be mass-produced by PR experts or self-help gurus.

- Watch out against any preacher, writer, seer, psychic or prophet whose message in the end is that your will and mind must be subjugated to theirs.

- Be alert for any attempt to treat you as a passive-dependent person, that is, to regress you to the role of childish devotion and obedience.

- Be especially cautious about those who offer simple, black/white, either/or answers and solutions to life's essential complexities. I know it's a seductive approach in our present time of tremendous confusion and "shaking of the foundations," but in the end it founders on the rocks of reality.

On the positive side, here are what constitute some marks of a genuinely spiritual person or "way":

- A deep awareness of the way in which the visible, experienced universe both hides and at the same time reveals the invisible truths and powers lying behind, beneath, and interpenetrating it.

- A full commitment to the reality we call God or divine Spirit, the one who sustains these truths and powers and who has made us "wired" for communication with herself/himself.

- A profound sensitivity to and compassion for all living beings, from the human to the tiniest creatures of all. This compassion or loving-kindness, taught by all the great religious and spiritual disciplines, is the highest virtue of all.

- The realization that we are spiritual beings who currently are having an earthly experience but who are one day destined for immortality.

- The teaching that we are all here for a reason, for some specific task(s), for our own unique mission.

- A profound commitment to social justice and to the well-being not just of all our brothers and sisters but to the whole biosphere as well.

- The conviction that personal life is about growth, transformation, service to others and the building of what is meant by the Kingdom of God.

Spirituality can easily become another high-sounding term for what amounts to narcissism all over again. It can be perverted into a false quest for bizarre manifestations of "another world." It can certainly be ripped off commercially. On the other hand, fully understood and sincerely pursued, it holds the promise of a new era of human progress and understanding.

EMPHASIS ON SIN CREATES
LACKLUSTRE SPIRITUALITY

———————

I was a fairly normal teenager growing up in the east end of Toronto, a neighbourhood somewhat trendily called the Upper Beaches today. I liked team sports such as basketball, make-up hockey and touch rugby. Hiking and birdwatching were favourite hobbies then as now. But I will never forget the sheer joy and thrill of learning to read both Greek and Latin and then eventually of translating the classical masters for myself.

It seems perhaps a bookish or even snobbish thing to say, but it happens to be true. The experience of reading Homer's *Odyssey* and then Herodotus and all the others in the original Greek, and of dipping into Horace, Virgil, Caesar, Tacitus and company in Latin, brought an enormous pleasure that's difficult to compare with anything else. But the greatest thrill was that of encountering and wrestling with Plato for the first time at college.

Those familiar with his thought, presented through Socrates as his chief protagonist—whether from reading either the Greek or one of the better translations—will know instantly what I mean. There's a reason Plato's philosophy had such a huge influence upon the Hellenistic world of the centuries leading up to the Roman Empire and has played so large a role in shaping much of western thinking. Something about his vision was, and remains, sublime. He cared about ultimate issues.

Not that Plato is always right or beyond critique. Aristotle, his most famous pupil, had fundamental disagreements with the master. So have I. It's just that his basic thought, with its insistence that true reality is not what we perceive or guess it to be at all, that is, not simply the surface, material world and the objects of our senses, but a far deeper, unseen and more abiding essence and "beingness," uplifts and inspires the soul.

That explains Plato's tremendous appeal down the ages and why today, people like me, amidst all the shallowness, find he so often comes to mind. Plato cared and wrote more profoundly about the soul and hence about what is meant by the word "spirituality" than almost any other writer before or since. Drawing, like all thinkers, upon the wisdom of those who had gone before him—mostly from the religious beliefs and lore of ancient Egypt, via a movement known as Orphism—he taught the immortality of the inner core or soul of every person. His anthropology was the very opposite of our materialistic reductionism in which human beings are thought of principally as chance products of a mechanistic universe, whose behaviour is determined purely by genes and biochemical processes alone, and whose ultimate destiny is the silent dust.

What I found and still find so bracing and challenging in Plato as I ponder a fitting spirituality for myself and others at this peculiar moment in human evolution is this understanding of the true nature of our humanity. According to Plato, as we have seen, we are a combination of the animal and the divine. Because of the gift of self-reflective consciousness or rational soul, we are indeed unique, "a little lower than the angels." Our task, he taught, is to seek after and follow The Good by struggling to keep the proper balance between our lower and higher natures. Values like justice, compassion, truth and beauty are not simply conveniences for a moment but lie eternal "in the heavens."

You can find some of these same emphases in the New Testament, most notably in Paul's letters, but they are at times overshadowed by a seeming obsession with our overwhelming sin, depravity and our alleged "Fall" through the mythical Adam. In too many of the traditional services and readings and sermons in churches every Sunday, the theme of human sinfulness and the need for redemption from beyond to qualify for God's approval in this world and the next still sounds forth under the pretext of being supposed "Good News." It isn't, and it's not surprising that it leaves such a lacklustre spirituality in its wake.

There are moments, when attending an Anglican Eucharist, that I'm almost stunned by the number of times the congregants have to plead for forgiveness and mercy for "things done that we ought not to have done. . . ." Surely one confession of sins is enough. By then, presumably, God expects us to get up and get on with it. If you tell people often enough that they're "miserable sinners" and "not worthy to gather up the crumbs under Thy table," it's not that surprising that they feel, and then often act, as though they are. Christianity ends up being a religion of guilt and, significantly, of hierarchical control derived from that guilt.

There's a "better story" than that in Plato. It's actually there in the Bible, too. But the feebleness of the spiritual pulse in too many traditional congregations tells me it's not being told very loudly or very well.

WHAT IT MEANS TO "LOVE" ENEMIES

Like many of you, I am a news addict. While it can for some come close to being a vice, there's no virtue in an arbitrary refusal to pay attention to what's going on around us.

Those who, in the name of a higher spirituality, make themselves blind and deaf to the glories, follies and tragedies of the global village reported in the media risk losing their souls in a hell of isolation and selfishness. However, as we read our newspaper and tune in to TV or radio news—trying our best to be aware and informed—there are soul risks, too. The greatest of these is our being so flooded at times by the torrent of information that we ignore the much profounder issues behind the day's or week's events.

We often ignore the spiritual subtext. Thus, for example, it's easier to ponder a future with an American president trying to call the shots on everything from biological warfare to the environment or to file away how many more Palestinians and Israelis have been killed—in what can surely no longer be called the "Holy Land"—than it is to think about the fundamental causes of violence and discord.

We forget that the global picture is a projection on a large scale of what is going on inside every human being's heart. Every truly inspired prophet, poet and visionary has made it plain that the causes of and solutions to every human problem, whatever its scale might be, lie in the heart and mind of each individual member of our species.

The spiritual giants of all time agree: If we want a world free of hatred, greed and injustice, we must begin by clearing our own inner lives of enmity and greed, and we must stop condoning those injustices, however small, that secretly benefit us. This can be hard soul-work and requires diligence and prayer as we do our part.

One of the most powerful visions of how this can happen comes from the most original, and most challenging, pronouncement attributed to Jesus Christ. It is found in the group of sayings in Matthew's Gospel known as the Sermon on the Mount (chapters 5–7, especially chapter 5:43–8) and boldly commands us to "love our enemies."

Yes, we've heard those words before, but take a few moments and really let them sink in. Never in the history of the world has a radical moral principle been formed and enunciated more clearly or potently than this. Yet never, through all the centuries since, has humanity rejected any commandment, principle or rule more fully— even more enthusiastically—than this.

One is reminded of the old adage: "It's not that Christianity has been tried and has failed. The problem is that it has never been truly tried at all." Certainly, Christians have never been found leading the charge, so to speak, when love of enemies has been required, with the possible exception of the Quakers and Mennonites. From my long familiarity with the many tensions in local congregations and with all that goes under the general tab of "church politics," it indeed seems that many would-be Christians have a tough enough time trying to love their friends, never mind possible foes!

This is far from a light matter, however. News items about road rage, air rage and all the other forms of societal rage reveal that there is often a seething cauldron of hate at the heart level that sooner or later is acted out collectively in vaster arenas. There are two things to remember. The first is that behind the Christian saying we should love and not hate our enemies, there is a powerful spiritual law according to which we tend to become like the object of our hatred. In other words, one must be careful who or what he/she hates because somehow, in this hot fixation of emotions, the hatred recoils on the hater.

The second thing to keep in mind is that the word in the Greek for "love" of enemies is the same word the New Testament uses for love of God or neighbour. It doesn't mean anything sentimental;

it has more to do with respecting and willing the very best for the other. For example, to love your neighbour or your enemy in this sense doesn't mean you necessarily have to like them. In the Christ Story, Jesus doesn't say: Like your enemies; pray for your persecutors. He says: Get rid of the hatred; wish for them what you wish for yourself; pray for true repentance for both parties.

As we absorb the daily news, we often wish we could change the world. And we can, by beginning at home. Carl Jung once wrote, at the height (or perhaps we should say depth) of the cold war, that it would take only the slightest change in the stability of the minds of leaders with access to the "nuclear button" to plunge the world into chaos and annihilation. His saying can be reversed. It would take only a slight change in the minds and hearts of Earth's total of billions of people to shift the balance towards global peace, justice and ecological renewal. That's what spiritual renewal is about.

HELL

———————

There are few ideas in history that have caused more misery, cruelty or misunderstanding than the concept of a fiery, eternal "place" called hell. Hell should be rejected on biblical and moral grounds—it's a major stumbling block to the growing number of spiritual seekers inside and outside the church.

With the abolition of hell, of course, purgatory goes too. It has no scriptural foundation and represents an attempt by institutions to retain power over members not only while they're living but beyond the grave as well. Belief in purgatory has kept millions in fear for centuries and created a lucrative industry in the process—masses on behalf of the dead, and so forth.

The central question raised by all of this, however, is: Does everybody, then, including the wicked, "go to heaven," and, if so, what has happened to God's justice? Before attempting to deal with that, though, first let's discuss heaven a little. Unfortunately, the traditional, popular notions of heaven promoted by institutional Christianity are almost as great a blockage to belief for contemporary spiritual seekers as the teachings about hell.

Mark Twain felt the necessity of politely, albeit satirically, refusing "God's Great Hereafter." He said he did so on the grounds that there was only so much milk and honey and so much angelic singing, punctuated by endless homilies, that he could stand! One would have to agree. Streets of gold and eternal choirs, together with all the rest of the rich but off-putting symbolism traditionally still used in hymns and sermons, don't really communicate the fullness of joy and the quality of existence the word "heaven" was originally intended to describe. Taken literally, the imagery then becomes boring, even banal. A tragedy.

The original Greek words translated as "eternal life" in the King James Version and many others mean simply, the "life of the age to come." In other words, while it will be an everlasting life, the emphasis is not on an infinite duration of time—after all, to be in God's presence is to be outside of time completely. Instead, the focus is on a certain quality of living in that new dimension. It will be bliss surpassing anything we have known, although I believe we have been given glimpses of it in the phenomenon known as the near-death experience (NDE).

Being in the new dimension called heaven will not be some static existence where all have won and all shall have the same prizes. From the NDE, from the teachings of other faiths and from such Bible passages as "in my Father's house are many mansions or dwelling places," I believe that in the life beyond death we continue to grow or "journey" spiritually. The word for "mansions" or "dwelling places" in the Greek is *monai,* meaning "way stations" or places to rest while on a journey. We don't arrive perfect or get zapped into perfection, as in a fantasy. We will start in heaven from different places.

But to return to our question: Who gets to transcend death and be received into the dimension of being that the word "heaven" attempts to describe? There are largely ignored parts of the New Testament that strongly suggest that, when all is wrapped up, everyone is received there, the wicked and even the monsters of history, as well as the just and the compassionate.

Those who build their beliefs about life to come on such verses and upon the overall picture of God's infinite mercy towards his created "children" given in most major faith traditions are called Universalists. They hold that in the end there will be no empty chairs, no ultimate frustrations of God's plan to bring all of humanity to the divine presence and glory.

Is there then no justice, no final morality, no ultimate difference between right and wrong? Yes, of course. World religions are virtually unanimous in their differently expressed conviction that the universe is supremely a place where justice and compassion matter. We are each of us responsible beings who will one day know and feel the consequences of every wrong act and utterance. There is judgment upon the least and upon the greatest, upon the hypocrite as well as upon the honestly pious.

The NDE provides an example of this in the stage known as the "life review" or being "judged by the Light." Reports of millions who have brushed the borders of death and returned testify to a part of the experience that is anything but cuddly or cozy. They tell of being in the presence of a great light (reminiscent of some sayings of Christ) where the whole of their lives pass before them. They see for the first time the depth of the hurt they have caused for themselves but especially for loved ones and others.

The intense and often excruciatingly painful exposure to such self-knowledge and the true implications of its full effects on others doesn't feel like condemnation from an angry God, they report. Rather, it's like being in a terribly revealing glare where nothing can be hidden any more. The torturer is forced to look into his victims' eyes and see the real suffering for the first time. The Hitlers and Stalins will be made to know without limit the unthinkable horrors they have wrought.

Yet, in the finale, even they will be drawn by God's love into the Kingdom of God. Both God's justice and God's mercy will be vindicated.

EVEN TODAY, MILLIONS OF PEOPLE
LIVE IN MORTAL FEAR OF SATAN

"What is the role of Satan in the Christian faith?" This was one of the first questions I received following a column I wrote on understanding the importance of atheists in the overall scheme of things. It's an important issue because even today there are millions who live in mortal fear of Satan, the devil, or, as they call "him" in Ireland, "Auld Clutey."

Extremists in Islamic as well as Christian circles are wont to label as satanic whatever influence, force or figure is deemed worthy of excoriation at any particular time. Jews, at least in my reading and experience, say little on the subject even though Satan (as one of the sons of God in the opening of the Book of Job) occurs in the Old Testament, too.

In the New Testament, Satan plays the role of adversary to the Christ. He tempts him in the visionary allegory of the temptation in the wilderness, and at least one Gospel makes it plain that this fictional account is only a window on what was conceived of as a continuous running battle throughout Jesus' ministry right up to the cross (Luke 4:13, Satan then left him "for a season"). The betrayal of Jesus by Judas is depicted as the result of Satan "entering into him" (John 13:27).

Satan, in a mythological sense, is really the alter ego of Jesus. In the ancient Egyptian parallel, the Christ figure and his opposite are set forth as twin brothers. This holds the esoteric or hidden key to the entire meaning of Satan's nature and function vis-à-vis the human condition.

Step back for a moment. Looking at the larger picture of the physical universe, we see at once that life is only possible—

the cosmos itself is only feasible—through a delicate balancing of polarities. If the moon were any farther away from Earth than it is, it would rush off into another orbit entirely. If it were any closer, the tides would be so colossal they would overwhelm much of the planet at every pull. One could go on, but the point is clear. Everything down to the slightest detail is in a delicate balance with everything else, the yin and yang of life.

But, and this is important, the polarities of up and down, hot and cold, light and dark, wet and dry, smooth and rough, painful and pleasurable, and so on, reflect on the natural plane what is true on the emotional, mental, moral and spiritual plane as well. We live between the polar opposites of good and evil, godly and ungodly, uplifting and degrading, light and shadow. Remarkably, perhaps, but truly nonetheless, any moral or spiritual growth is only possible when we are caught up by our thoughts and actions in the tension between these opposites. In making our way forward, true progress flows from the dynamic fuelled by the grinding or meshing of the two magnetic-like attractors as they interface within us.

Satan, then, is a metaphor or symbol of the lower force. Christ, or whatever other name or symbol operates best for you, represents that of the higher life. Make no mistake, these polar opposites may have metaphorical names, they may be images or symbols, but they refer to mighty psychic realities or powers in our innermost lives.

There certainly is no literal devil with all the paraphernalia centuries of warped superstition and bad religion have decked him out with. Martin Luther may have thrown his inkwell at him once in a fit of fear and/or rage, but there was no creature with horns and a pitchfork and cloven feet. There was no actual figure of evil standing beside or before Jesus in the story of the temptation. The scene is from a drama of the soul.

You may say: "But what about the many stories in the Gospels, especially the earliest, that of Mark, about Jesus casting devils or demons out of sundry sick folks." The reply to that is that any story told in that time of a prophet who didn't include exorcisms of this type in his repertoire would scarcely have been listened to by those expecting such signs. The fact that there are stories in the Bible about healing demon possession doesn't necessitate believing that any historical Jesus believed in demons or cast them out. The inner meaning is that the Christ consciousness within can help rid us of crippling negativities.

If somebody is so deluded or ill as to believe they have been possessed by the devil, the best tack a healer can take is to deal directly with the problem as presented. In a story once told of Dr. Norman Bethune, he showed students how, when a patient is possessed by the belief that he has swallowed a live frog, it can work wonders to slip one into the bedpan at an appropriate moment following a purgative medication.

In general, then, "Satan" stands for those forces that oppose the good but in doing so help make being good the victory it is.

WHO GOES TO HEAVEN?

There was a headline right across the top of a page in the Good Friday *Star* that gave me a sudden inner tug. The years rolled away and I was a small boy again for a moment—a child faced with a deeply haunting fear. The headline, which was over a half-page Religious News Service wire story, screamed out: "Who exactly gets into heaven?"

Strange to tell, that question in various forms frightened me for much of my early youth. The deep anxiety around it came from my own parents', and their friends' deep and steady commitment to an answer that was so very narrow that it excluded most of my friends and their parents—not to mention the rest of the world.

Though we were Anglicans and I once sang as a boy chorister in an Anglican church choir, when I was between age nine and fourteen we attended a deeply conservative evangelical church where hellfire and damnation were constantly proclaimed. The Battle of Armageddon was a frequent sermon theme. Only the "saved"—strictly defined as born-again, former sinners—were going to escape the horrors to come. The urgent duty of each member was to avoid contact with those "who belong to this world" while at the same time—paradoxically—getting to know such worldings well enough to "lead them to Christ."

They were there to be "snatched as brands from the burning to come." Naturally, like every other kid whose family belonged to this assembly—housed in a basement-like structure on Victoria Park Avenue in Toronto's east end—I spent a lot of time worrying. I worried whether my grandparents in Ireland who went to church but seemed to care little or nothing about being "saved" would manage to make it. Would my best friend, John Cunningham, who once kept my pet white rat while we were on holiday in Ireland, roast in hell? He didn't care a fig about religion but was great at birdwatching and building fires in some back lane to roast our "borrowed" potatoes.

I prayed constantly for the unsaved, especially the huge motor-cycle cop who would often turn up in full uniform on our doorstep for a sudden visit. He usually carried a mickey of whisky tucked down inside one of his leather leg guards. I remember the sad look in his eyes as my mother regularly pounced on it and poured the contents down the sink while delivering a sermon of her own.

My sister and I left salvation "tracts" in phone booths and else-where and dreaded the times when we were taken to local street-corner meetings where "the Gospel was proclaimed" while we prayed our friends wouldn't spot us taking part.

Thank God, we gradually were able to grasp and hammer out a more mature, inclusive understanding of the divine mysteries. My father eventually studied theology, then quit his secular job and was ordained as an Anglican priest. He passed his new insights to my mother and indirectly to the rest of the family. (My own education in classics and theology was as yet to unfold.) Little by little we were able to "put away childish things," to quote St. Paul, and look with profound trust to God to bring us and all his/her children on the face of the Earth into the fold.

I received a letter just recently from an angry reader denouncing me in shocked tones as a universalist. That's really a compliment in my estimation. The term, as we've seen, refers to one who holds that in the final reckoning all will be "saved," that is, all will "go to heaven" or come in full glory into the divine Presence. Not that any of us is ready for that yet. Whatever we mean by heaven, it is not some silent mortuary of "perpetual rest." We all of us have so much to learn, so much growing yet to do, such vast vistas of deep under-standing to explore. But one day the promise to each is that we shall know even as we are known. We know in part only now, but then "face to face."

The striking thing is that this universalist type of understanding is far from being some new, liberal creed. The doctrine that ultimately all free moral creatures, "angels, humans and devils," to quote the *Oxford Dictionary of the Christian Church,* will share in the grace of salvation was called "apocatastasis," or restoration, in ancient Greek. It is to be found in the doctrines of Clement of Alexandria, in Origen, and St. Gregory of Nyssa, three of the most brilliant of the earliest Fathers of the Church. But it was—like so much that was good—later condemned as a heresy.

I believe they were right. At the last, there will be no empty chairs at what is called metaphorically the wedding feast of heaven. Who gets into heaven? Finally, everyone.

OUR CAPACITY FOR GOODNESS
IS REALLY INFINITE

———————————

Recently, we noticed our large male cat, Cheddar, sitting at the fireplace staring raptly through the glass doors. After a while, I went to see what was of such absorbing interest. Nothing stirred. But still he sat and watched. Later on, we found out why. A bird had come down the chimney and was trapped. Susan held the cat while I opened the front door. Then I opened the fireplace doors. The bird flew directly out of the house and vanished. Cheddar, however, missed its exit and remains sure it's still there. Even today, several days afterwards, he spent hours by the hearth patiently waiting for that bird to show up.

Part of the charm of animals lies in this purity of purpose. They are what they are without guile. They are never untrue to their own nature. The human animal is a very different story. After hundreds of thousands of years of evolution, *Homo sapiens* remains a mystery to himself, a set of contradictions; part saint, part devil. Unlike other animals, what you see is not always what you get. As Shakespeare says in *Measure for Measure*:

> O, what may man within him hide,
> Though angel on the outward side!

We can answer that quite easily by reading our daily newspaper. Just when you think you have read of every cruelty, outrage, folly and filthiness conceivable—things which St. Paul describes as "too shameful even to mention"—you find that there is some new twist to our capacity for evil. Killing, torture, betrayal, abuse of innocence, rape and bloody assault, rapacious greed, jealousy and lies unending. The catalogue is staggering.

However, the capacity for goodness is also virtually infinite. While not reported with the same eager fascination, the quiet heroism, self-giving, generosity, courage, faithfulness, courtesy and sheer love exhibited by millions upon millions of ordinary people every moment of every day around the planet vastly exceeds any final tally of injustice, savagery or other wickedness. To quote Shakespeare again:

> What a piece of work is man! How noble in reason!
> How infinite in faculty . . . in action how like an angel!

This paradox of human nature can be illustrated by the human hand. As a piece of engineering and kinetic design it surpasses all our sophisticated technology. It can play music that can move us to tears. It can operate on the human brain or paint a masterpiece. It is the universal agent of untold giving and caring and healing and love. But with it Cain held the rock that killed his brother, Abel. The hand is the chief tool of all violence and inhumanity to others. If, God forbid, a nuclear war were ever to be launched, it would begin by the touch of a human hand, a finger on the button of an apocalypse.

The most tempting and hence prevalent response to this deep dichotomy in the human soul is denial. Like most denial it masks itself from us—we see the evil as "out there" or as belonging to others quite alien to ourselves. It's a product of succumbing too easily to the either/or approach critiqued in my columns before. People are either all good or all bad in this view. Naturally, we are on the side of the pure. Those who commit the crimes which so disgust us are "not like us."

This perspective may be comforting but it's an illusion. Belief in it does nothing to help us understand evil either in others or in ourselves. In fact, the failure to face up to the extent to which this dual nature of our humanity is deeply embedded in every one of us is a major source of the species' slowness to make moral progress. There is what Dr. Carl Jung called "the shadow" within the unconscious depths of every individual. There is no evil known of which we are not every one of us capable.

Over-indignation and shocked finger-pointing at the crimes of others often testifies to our terror of the darkness inside; it's a way of trying to avoid our own shadow. We think self-knowledge is fine up to a point, but there are parts of our soul we firmly refuse to know. There's a price to be paid for this. Because we won't recognize our own particular shadow, we fail to comprehend the darkness of humanity's collective shadow and both individually and globally go on to make the same mistakes.

THE MORAL LAW WITHIN
IS A GIFT FROM GOD

———————

Crime and Punishment, by Fyodor Dostoyevski (1821–1881), is one of the most powerful novels ever written. Among other deep issues, it wrestles with the fundamental ethical question: Why be good? Why not commit murder, theft, adultery, lying, betrayal of others or any number of other sins in the catalogue of vice?

What is the final motivation, reason or point of pursuing a virtuous life when other options are open—possibly more pleasurable or more immediately to one's own gain or advantage over others? Where does the near-universal sense of obligation to act in an ethical fashion derive its potency in spite of all our human weakness and propensity for evil?

Fear of punishment, either by God or by assorted systems of justice, has compelled millions in the past to maintain at least a public veneer of virtue. For centuries, the fear of a hell to come and the fear of brutal chastisement from various authorities were sufficient to keep many on the straight and narrow who would otherwise have strayed.

While religion wielded the stick of eternal torment for those who forsook goodness, it offered as well the carrot of heavenly rewards for those who earnestly sought to toe the line. As the power of organized religion wanes today, however, neither fear of hell nor cupidity for golden crowns hereafter have much continuing clout.

In any case, hope of eternal gain or dread of future pain are not sufficiently cogent moral reasons for seeking goodness. The person holding no belief in any form of afterlife would presumably then feel justified in acting just as she or he pleased. But atheists and agnostics can and do achieve goodness also. Believers have no monopoly on it. Rewards and appropriate punishments can be used in training the young, and they may well be the only way a stable society can administer itself. However, there will always be those who, if that is the only basis for "being good," can argue to themselves that it's really "not getting caught" that counts.

In *Crime and Punishment*, one of the oldest theories of all gets a thorough working over, that is, that morality and goodness are simply a plot by the great majority who are weak to keep the strong at bay. For a while, the central character, Raskalnikov, a young man who murders an old woman and steals her money, gets carried away with the idea that the truly strong person is the one who has the courage to make his own rules. Goodness is for the feeble.

This kind of "law of the jungle" amorality soon lies exposed in the novel for the nihilistic and chaotic lie it is. True, there always have been, and perhaps always will be, individuals, groups and nations who act on this excuse for a code, whatever their public pretences. But they have always invoked some other moral basis of action from those they feared. It's like the bully who cries "fight fair" to an aggressor stronger than himself.

The argument that we should be good, law-abiding, virtuous citizens because it's useful or conducive to the greatest happiness of the greatest number has always had a powerful attraction for many. But the equation *good equals useful* simply doesn't stand up to closer scrutiny.

There have always been those—I believe today they're a majority—who have within themselves a moral vision that includes sometimes doing that which is not just the approved or obviously "useful" thing in a particular situation because they feel their plain duty is to act otherwise. They act against all public or private pressure to do differently because of an inner conviction that the right or good compels them whatever the cost.

In other words, wherever true goodness shows itself in a heroic or an exemplary way, often accompanied by personal loss or some form of sacrifice by the doer, it becomes clear that some standard other than a utilitarian social contract (agreement of the majority as to what is useful) is operating.

There is an inner law written in the hearts and consciences of humans which, however sensitive it may be to external influences—law codes, sacred books, religious figures—is the final arbiter and raison d'être of goodness and our feeling of "oughtness" about being good.

What Immanuel Kant (1724–1804) called "the moral law within," a reality that never ceased to fill his mind with "ever-increasing wonder and awe," is a gift of God and of the universe to each of us. We strive to follow it not for gain or out of fear but because it is only by doing so that we can be true to our deepest selves.

Ultimately, there is no valid reason for being good other than sheer goodness itself.

THE DECISION TO GROW
IS ALL OUR OWN

———————

Somewhere recently, while driving, I caught a small sign or piece of graffiti out of the corner of my eye which read: "Change is inescapable; growth is a matter of choice." Since both ethics and spirituality are supremely concerned with growth and with choice, this maxim has been simmering in my mind ever since.

The question which has finally crystallized is simple but crucial, not just for parents or others entrusted with the training of the young, but for every one of us: How do we measure moral and spiritual development? What are the marks of progress so that we can tell when we or others are indeed growing and not standing still or sliding backwards?

Let's be clear about one thing first, though. I'm not talking about becoming more religious. Ideally, religion is about right conduct and a deepening inner or spiritual life. In reality, however, we know from history, from just looking around us, or from reading the newspaper that very religious people can often be spiritual and ethical dwarves. There are many parts of the world today that need more religion like the Sahara needs more sand!

I'm not against religion. It's just that one can never underestimate the need to distinguish between religiosity and spirituality, between the world of external piety or rituals and that of true morality. They don't necessarily coincide.

Because the life of the spirit and one's morality or values are intimately connected, there's bound to be overlap in any attempt to examine them. Having said that, let's look first at some criteria for spiritual growth. This brief list is not set out in any order of priority.

Indeed, each of us will have our own priorities and these can change as we mature.

- *Self-knowledge:* If I know no more about myself today—my weaknesses, my strengths, my deepest allurements, my profoundest hopes for myself and others, my greatest fears—than I did six months or a year ago, I have not grown. We are experts at self-deception and at self-justification. There's no growth where there's no ongoing effort to remove all the masks and face our inner truth.

- *Cosmic connectedness:* Spirituality involves a sense of meaning and of purpose beyond the biological and materialistic. This can only flow from an understanding of one's belonging to or having an intimate place in the cosmic picture. Is it getting stronger?

- *Depth awareness:* Is our sensitivity to beauty, suffering, the natural world and the invisible energies flowing through us and those around us becoming sharper, more aware? Or are we settling for the mere surface of living? The Higher Self longs for "soul" or depth.

Criteria for judging ethical growth must include at least the following:

- *Compassion:* Strikingly, in today's neo-conservative, bottom-line social climate, some of the people who parrot family values as a slogan are trying simultaneously to make compassion almost a dirty word. This flatly contradicts the moral wisdom of all major religions and philosophies. Compassion is the heart of ethics. Not to grow in it is to miss the real point of being truly human.

- *A sense of social justice:* Increasing commitment to justice for everyone, particularly the weakest, the poorest and the most oppressed—also including animals and Earth itself—ranks beside compassion as a moral norm for judging our own and others' growth. The world cries out for it.

- *Devotion to truth in word and life:* You can't go on living a lie and pretend or hope you are growing morally. You can't go about telling lies and so-called half-truths and assume blithely that this does no soul damage within and little harm to others. Deceit is incompatible with either spiritual or moral progress.

- *Seeing and treating others as subjects, never as objects:* The major pressures of modern life tilt us towards the "thingification" of those outside our closest circle—and even of those within it. Integrity in sexuality, in business, in every relationship, in every aspect of living depends upon the extent to which we see other persons as subjects in their own dignity and right rather than as objects for our use, pleasure, profit or control. We are either becoming more sensitive to this key dimension or less, and a world of difference lies between.

We need to pray as though it all depends on God, but to work at it as though it all depends on us. That's the secret. We can do nothing to stop change, but personal growth is in our hands. It's what we choose and then do that counts.

HEALING AND THE COSMIC CONNECTION

———————

Over the years I have been committed to researching spiritual heal-ing. One thing that has impressed me deeply, especially in looking at both ancient and aboriginal approaches, is the role played in other cultures by the "cosmic dimension" in human health. It's a factor virtually absent from today's medicine. More significantly, it's lacking in every other aspect of our lives as well. The results are destructive.

We have three basic dimensions as humans: the individual, the social, and the cosmic—that is, how we relate to ourselves, to oth-ers, and to the universe or the totality itself. Though we may scarcely ever give it a thought, this latter aspect, the cosmic, is of vast impor-tance to our overall health and sense of well-being. As the eminent physicist David Bohm has said: "From the earliest times it has been considered crucial, for the overall order of the individual and soci-ety, that a harmonious relationship be established with this whole (the universe)."

One of the chief functions of the shaman, medicine man or other healers who have appeared in every corner of the globe back to the dawn of time was/is to help the diseased or troubled to restore this cosmic harmony. Ultimately, wholeness was seen as profoundly dependent upon knowing one's place in the cosmic drama, one's kinship with the universe and all life. As Bohm points out in *Science, Order, and Creativity,* in former ages the two chief ways in which humans kept their cosmic awareness alive were through their deep immersion in nature and through religion. Today, however, since most people live in sprawling urban settings far from nature, and since religion's influence has greatly diminished, this sense of cos-mic connectedness has all but vanished.

In earlier times, the urgent sense of the wider environment—the winds, the sky, the undulating fields, the rivers, lakes and oceans, the cycle of the seasons and the starry canopy of the night sky—was a constant reminder of the need for an adjustment to and an understanding of the whole. Today, with our endless malls and climate-controlled dwellings, our cars, ubiquitous cellphones, and all the other fruits of technology about us, we live unmindful of the deeper rhythms and bonds between us and the overarching, cosmic reality. Similarly, as religion has ceased to be the major source of ultimate meaning for millions, the old rituals aimed at linking us with the universe and the Source of all things have lost their impact. Science fills the gap for some. In spite of all its successes, however, science is much too fragmented and often too esoteric in its language and symbols to be helpful. It only deals with one dimension. As I mentioned in *The Uncommon Touch: An Investigation of Spiritual Healing*, more than sixty million North Americans a year confirm, by their use of nonconventional therapies, that the present scientific approach to health is far too narrow. They rightly believe we are much more than mind-body machines.

The loss of this sense of where and how one belongs in the cosmos has had disastrous effects upon western society. It's one of the chief sources of the general neurosis of meaninglessness that pervades our consumer-driven culture. Lives do not and cannot make final sense when they exist in a kind of limbo, detached from the sum of the processes and the total setting which gave them birth. Even many experts on human behaviour and the social problems that plague us—mindless violence, addictions of every kind, suicides and the endemic sense of stress—seem blind to the deeper causes of our illness.

The widespread angst and loss of meaning are not consciously related by most to this underlying lack of connectedness to the whole. We look feverishly everywhere else for answers.

This absence of a cosmic connection blocks our creativity and our ability to find the kind of solutions to global problems so urgently needed at this time. We cannot deal with the planetary crises—wars, the problem of the haves and the have-nots or the ecological night-mare—unless and until we can break through to a cosmic conscious-ness in the light of which everything else can flow together. Since we cannot turn the clock back and return to a life completely immersed in nature and the elements (nature has been so badly degraded that even that experience would no longer be the same), and since tradi-tional religions have become increasingly irrelevant in a secularized world, the paramount question is: How can a vital understanding of one's place in the cosmos be realized? If it is essential to whole-ness, how can we be "healed"?

The answer ultimately is a spiritual one. If present faiths don't meet this challenge, through inaction or stupidity, they will wither away and a fresh wind of the Spirit will blow. We are spiritual beings in a cosmos made and sustained by God. That alone is the truth that can make us free—and whole. It's a pearl of great price indeed.

5

TRANSFORMATION

Though I take the wings of the morning and dwell in the uttermost parts of the Earth, Behold you are there also.

— PSALM 139:9

WE ARE NEVER REALLY GOD-FORSAKEN

Few things in the gamut of human experience can surpass the pain and desolation of feeling overwhelmed by loneliness and deep depression. Whatever the root cause, the terrible loss of a loved one, some acute and devastating public failure, an act of shame, a betrayal or abandonment of monumental proportions, or perhaps hereditary brain chemistry itself, at times the pangs of God-forsakenness can threaten to topple the fortress of the soul.

A friend who recently, after a serious heart attack, found himself in Intensive Care feeling disoriented, frightened out of his wits and experiencing for the first time just how much on our own we all are when this reality suddenly sinks in, described his sense of undergoing "an amputated spirit." Call it what you will, it comes to us all one day. For some it is a never-ending nightmare, a total dark night of the soul.

Paradoxically, what I'm describing happens most often to the most sensitive in our midst. Certainly those seeking hardest to try to live a spiritual path have left us a rich literature as testimony to the fact that being a believer is no insurance against such agony. Martin Luther suffered depression. The recently published diaries of Mother Teresa reveal the same. Indeed, one could almost argue that such seasons of "dryness" seem an essential ingredient in the struggle to encounter and know the divine dimension of our being more fully.

It is striking that the chilling words (the "cry of dereliction") from Psalm 22, "My God, my God, why have you forsaken me?" are put into the mouth of Jesus in Mark and Matthew's version of the crucifixion. As the central character in the potent drama of the human soul, in matter he must be shown to have endured and voiced this most awful of our Incarnation's woes.

Thinking of this, and knowing how full some people's lives are of lesser Calvaries at this moment, led me back recently to the most favourite of all my favourite Psalms—Psalm 139. Down the years it has echoed constantly in my mind when I or others near me have passed close to or through the valley of the shadow. I use it whenever I need to be truly inspired. What's so moving in this ancient yet always timely soliloquy of one man's soul is its radical honesty and its scouring depth of insight. The words of the King James Version (KJV) are magnificent and familiar, but for contemporary meaning the New Revised Standard Version is nearer the mark.

I hope that you, whether you are a person of faith (any faith) or not, will pick up a copy of the Psalter or entire Bible and read the poem through—perhaps more than once. In verses 1 to 6, the Psalmist muses on the way in which God knows him, his thoughts, his words before they leave his tongue, his passage through the coils of living, even his sitting down and his rising up.

Then at verse 7, he reveals his real starting point, the reasons for his reverie. He has obviously been aware of that feeling spoken of already, that all-too-human sense of desolation and of "amputated" spirit where the head may think of God but the heart feels deserted, lonely and bereft.

He cries: "Where can I go from your spirit? Or where can I flee from your presence?" Then comes a resounding answer in peal after peal of affirmation and saving hope. The realization sweeps in that feelings or no feelings—no matter what transpires—God's presence is inescapable. The Psalmist's emotions may be one thing, but the bedrock truth is another. He says: "If I ascend to heaven, you are there; if I make my bed in hell, you are there."

Then, in some of the loveliest phrases in the Bible, he says that if he were to "take the wings of the morning" and settle at the farthest limits of the ocean "even there your hand shall lead me and your right hand shall hold me fast." Even if he were to imagine that his soul's darkness might cover him and the night of depression hide him from his God, he says, even that utter gloom would make not one iota of difference "for darkness is as light to you."

Being no saint, he vents a little hot hatred of his enemies in four verses (19 to 22). These resound meaningfully to me only when I take them metaphorically as his attitude to his inner demons. But the ending is a beautiful, useful prayer. I call it prayer "with suction."

The overall message? We are never really God-forsaken. Feelings cannot be ignored. They do matter—but certainly at times they also can deceive.

WE CANNOT
AVOID GOD'S QUESTIONS

Since it's almost entirely poetry and "true myth," and since we live in one of the most literal-minded cultures of all time, it's not surprising that the Bible largely remains a closed book. Those who make the loudest claims for its veracity often see its meaning less clearly than many they judge to be total outsiders. If you treat biblical myths as history, you end up with either distortion or absurdity. Even worse. As Voltaire once said: "Those who believe absurdities end up committing atrocities."

When read for what it genuinely is, the story—told in myths, parables, metaphors and allegory—of the evolution of the human soul and its relationship to the mystery called God, the wider human community and the cosmos itself, its power for inspiration and transformation is immeasurable.

For example, everybody recognizes that the two accounts in the opening chapters of Genesis which tell of the creation and of the beginnings of the human saga are mythical in nature. They have to be. There is simply no other way of expressing such sublime truths as they contain. The packaging is fictional, but the inner, abiding truth being told is eternal.

Properly understood, they put a finger on the very core of our being. They touch our life today, now, in this moment. Here is a simple example. After Adam and Eve had tasted the forbidden fruit (nothing whatever to do with either apples or sex, by the way), they tried to hide from God: "And they heard the voice of the Lord God walking in the garden in the cool of the day: and Adam and his wife hid themselves from the presence of the Lord God amidst the trees of the garden."

Then rings out a question that has come echoing down the centuries with a never-ceasing urgency to each of us: "And the Lord God called unto Adam [the word means, simply, man in the generic sense] and said unto him, 'Where art thou?'"

We try to hide from God—from the true depths of ourselves and of our beingness—and the haunting, searching question keeps on coming in so many varied, sometimes subtle, sometimes shrieking, ways: "Where are you?"

We are challenged to pause and consider, to ask ourselves where we really are in our lives, where we are in our intentions, in our relationships, in our spiritual journey, in our own personal evolution, in our connection with our Higher Self and with others.

Anyone who equates myth with fairy tales or assumes that because no Adam and Eve ever existed as objective, historical entities, the entire creation account can be dismissed or ignored is self-deceived. The eternal truth is there and cannot be denied. The Ground of All Being hurls this question at us: "Where are you right now?" And the universe awaits the answer.

Different Bible myths confront the soul within us with other profound questions that strike equally at the meaning and fabric of our daily existence, if only we pay attention. I'm thinking in particular of a passage from the stories in the First Book of Kings (chapter 19) about the great prophet Elijah. It's dealt with in detail in *Finding the Still Point* but sounds within as a frequent check on my own spiritual growth—or lack of it—and so comes to mind powerfully here.

Because many people feel at times depressed, frustrated, weary or burned out, they can identify with Elijah's plight. Even though he had accomplished great things and had seen God acting in his life, he found himself at one point quite down—even to the point of longing for death itself. He tries to wiggle and twist and, like Adam, to escape somehow rather than boldly face his situation. He takes refuge in a cave. Then comes the divine Questioner with this probing query: "What are you doing here, Elijah?"

In other words, he has reached a point in his life where he has to stop and take a very long, hard look at what on earth he is really doing with it. Where is he headed? Why is he at this particular spot in it? What is really going on? Confrontation with this crisis brings him a fresh vision of God in that "still, small voice" that speaks to him and commissions him for fresh directions, new challenges. He is changed, transformed, turned from defeat to a person throbbing with energies for greater achievements still.

Life today seduces us into thinking that these and the other life-changing questions posed by the Bible can be avoided by sheer busyness, the never-ending quest for pleasure or other forms of running away to hide. But, like Francis Thompson's Hound of Heaven, in his poem by that name, they ever pursue us, silently. Waking or sleeping, they follow us "down the labyrinthine ways" of our own hearts and minds, and call for an answer.

WHEN WE FEEL THE
ABSENCE OF GOD IN OUR LIVES

————————

I received a letter recently from one of the most energetic and keen Christian leaders I have known. He thanked me for a column on the use of stillness in one's spiritual life. It seems he had been going through a difficult time and feeling discouraged. Reading between the lines, it was clear to me he has been experiencing a phenomenon which people of all faiths who are sincere seekers sooner or later—and more frequently for some—come to know intimately. This experience can be very intense. The mystics call that the "dark night of the soul."

In its milder forms it is best described as a period of spiritual and irrational "dryness." It feels like the absence of God. Prayers seem to mock one, bouncing back, as it were, from the ceiling. Some have described this aspect by saying "the heavens themselves seem made of brass." Or the soul becomes so lethargic and confused that one is unable to pray at all. Torpor sets in.

It can be reassuring to know that this is a universal fact, that no matter how saintly or spiritual a cleric or anybody else may be, no matter how fervently they talk about "knowing the Lord" or living the abundant life, they too have times when there is a void within. God, as the psalmist says, seems to "hide His face" and to be deaf to all entreaties. Instead of enjoying the divine Presence, one faces emptiness. The garden becomes a desert. And it is easy to falter.

Before too quickly assuming there is some ethical or spiritual problem blocking the Spirit's flow, a common-sense approach looks first at more practical matters, such as whether or not there is a way for repressed rage to be safely vented. But no matter how healthy one is or how good one's relationships with others may be, living a life of faith is no guarantee of sensing a perpetual oneness with and joy in the Creator. In fact, while it's wonderful to experience exalted emotions, and even perhaps occasionally ecstasy, living a spiritual path is not really a matter of feelings at all. It's a commitment of mind and will as well as of the heart. One believes because one knows it to be true. One stays obedient through good feelings and bad because *one wills to remain true* to the One who has promised to be faithful forever. The only effective way to deal with dryness or times of God's seeming absence is to keep at one's post, remembering both God's promises and past mercies—"until the night is gone." The shortest way out of this particular kind of wilderness is to go straight through. Winston Churchill put it with characteristic bluntness when he said, "KBO"—keep buggering on!

What I have experienced, however, and what every spiritual source I have ever read confirms, is that there is a paradoxical element in this process. The time of absence or of spiritual dryness often is seen, in retrospect, to have been the place where God's Presence was most clearly at work in our lives. One way of putting it is to say that when it comes to spiritual growth we learn far more and advance further during or just after the bleak periods than we do in the halcyon days when we are more or less on top of the world. God is not playing games with us. There is never a time when we are beyond God's care and love. But we have a desperate need to become more mature, more fully what we are designed to be, and that doesn't come by singing and dancing one's way through life.

I do not believe the loving Intelligence we call God ever sends grief, illness or spiritual dryness "to do us good." (To send evil that good may come is immoral, a version of the end justifying the means.) Rather, these things are simply facts of life. Properly understood and used, they can become wells of living water for the road ahead.

What we all-too-human believers experience as God's absence is really but a different modality or dimension of the Presence. By perseverance and trust we can find ourselves saying of any particular dry spell what Jacob said of a similar experience long ago. Having cheated his brother Esau twice, he was being hunted and was on the run. He found himself alone, in the dark, in the bare wilderness. Frightened and cold, he lay down with only a rock for a pillow. Then he had his famous dream, already cited in chapter 1, of the ladder going up to heaven and angels ascending and descending on it. Later, he awoke and said with great surprise: "Surely God was in this place and I knew it not!"

That can be our experience too. Today.

CHAOS AND CREATIVITY

———————

For twenty years we lived on the shore of a small lake about forty minutes drive north of Toronto. The lake was created as the glaciers from the last Ice Age receded over twelve thousand years ago. Sometimes, sitting at our campfire at night and seeing the gleam of others on a farther shore, we pretended these were Indian camps from long ago and that all around was wilderness. It gave one perspective in the morning to see a muskrat swimming by and Canada geese like phantom galleons in the dawn mist. Their ancestors did that there before the first cities were built in Mesopotamia, before any of the great moral codes were formed or the major world religions took shape.

Because of some science I have read lately, I've been watching something I never really noticed before. When a flock of geese, or other migratory birds, are startled or simply decide to take off, there's a brief time of apparent confusion and chaos. There's a furious whirring, splashing and crying; the air above the water is a blur of beating wings; nobody could conceivably predict by scientific means which bird will be where in the next fraction of a second. But very quickly a transformation occurs. What was a frantic mess is suddenly an emerging pattern. In seconds, a full and graceful order appears. They move as one. The same thing can be observed with schools of fish in the ocean and with a whole range of other phenomena in nature, from the formation of crystals to patterns in the weather.

Modern chaos theory in physics stresses that while science's main task in the past has been, and to a large extent still is, to discern order and laws in the universe, there are areas of wholly unpredictable, chaotic events where uncertainty reigns. You can see this by watching the shapes and movements of clouds in the sky, of the plumes of smoke from a cigarette, or of the foam below a rapids or falls. But it pervades the cosmos. The fascinating thing, however, is that this chaos, whether in the movement of grains of sand on a beach or asteroids in space, is creative. It holds within itself, as with the flying birds, the potential for a quickly emerging, higher order. There is, in other words, what scientists are now calling a principle or force of anti-chaos as well. From turmoil and confusion comes a richer design. This happened in the seconds, minutes and hours after the primeval "flaring forth" or Big Bang fifteen billion years ago when things began. It goes on today.

I believe that the Mind of God is the architect and the intelligence in, through and behind this incredibly mysterious and complex process. I believe also that what happens externally in the physical order happens also in the raw material of our lives. After all, we are part and parcel of the whole of nature. In other words, the forces of cosmos (order), chaos and anti-chaos are also at work in us. We have called them by other names in the past, but sometimes it helps to see them in another light. Cosmos, which comes from a Greek word meaning to bring order out of chaos (*kosmeo,* from which we get our word "cosmetics"!), is a gift from God and we all experience it to some degree: the ability to think or the times when life flows along more or less evenly; we know happiness at some or many levels; we do what we know to be right almost by instinct.

Few, if any, however, escape times of utter turmoil and chaos. These events can be triggered by unforeseen circumstances wholly beyond our control, for example, natural disasters, accidents, economic surprises, or illnesses and death of those most loved. They can be the result of our own ignorance, folly, idleness, meanness or weakness. Or they can come from a combination of some or all of the above. We have a sense of having lost direction or we have a feeling of being singled out for punishment by fate, destiny or God. One of the things I like most about the Book of Psalms in the Hebrew Bible, or Old Testament, is that the writer so often wrestles and sweats over this very problem. It's like what I described in an earlier column as a dark night of the soul.

Yet, experience has shown me that as in chaos theory one can almost always see in retrospect that the chaos held within itself the seeds of a new order about to emerge. It was not "sent" to teach or to punish, but it did hold a promise of better things to come. There was, one might say, a principle of anti-chaos deep within it which, had one looked for it earlier, one might have discerned then and so have gained hope and courage even in the midst of an emotional/ intellectual/physical or circumstantial mess. In spiritual terms, the Spirit of God is always "brooding over the waters" of our primal chaos to bring new order—as at the first creation.

To find this is to know with the Psalmist: "I waited patiently for the Lord and he inclined unto me and heard my calling. He took me up also out of the horrible pit, out of the mire and clay; and set my feet on a rock, and *ordered* my goings" (Psalm 40).

THE DARK NIGHT OF THE SOUL

———————

A Calgary journalist called me just before Christmas and arranged a phone interview for the next day. He wanted to talk about prayer. When the time came, we had an interesting forty-five minutes or so on the topic and then we talked more personally.

Like many people today—and throughout the ages—he said he was genuinely keen to deepen his spirituality but sometimes found himself tempted to abandon the quest because of apparent lack of progress. He went on to describe the difficulty of staying with regular meditation when it's so hard to still one's mind for any length of time. The so-called "monkey mind" is always chattering away. He spoke also of those periods of dryness of soul when prayers bounce back at us, the times we find ourselves repeating old habits of judging others, of not guarding against thoughtless conversation, or of expecting forgiveness from everybody else while giving none ourselves.

It was all so familiar. In my own experience. In the vast ranges of spiritual literature. In the lives of almost everyone I know or have known as a minister, then teacher, and in my present role. Nobody who truly seeks to know as he or she is already known by the Mind and Heart of the Universe can escape this kind of frustration, sense of defeat, or even at times despair—the "dark night of the soul."

I shared candidly with him what I have learned on my personal journey. Two key convictions have emerged: first, as already discussed, the total universality of the "spiritual discouragement" syndrome; he and I, and you perhaps, are not unique, alone, or different from others when we find that the spiritual path is often beset by difficulties.

Second, however, it is frequently, perhaps always, the case that such times of testing prove in the end to be much more productive of solid growth and fresh insights than when everything seems to flow in a stream of calm enjoyment. There is a spiritual principle or law laid down: out of weakness can come great strength.

Even a great spiritual warrior like the Apostle Paul knew times of dryness, weakness and near despair. But he tells us, "When I am weak, then am I strong"—through what he called the Christ within.

Here Hindu master Patanjali describes this same phenomenon from a Vedic perspective:

> When an aspirant enters upon the spiritual life, he naturally does so with great enthusiasm. The first steps . . . are almost always accompanied by feelings of peace and delight. Everything seems so easy, so inspiring. It is thus very important that he should realize, right from the start, that this mood will not continue, uninterrupted through the rest of his course. . . . There will be relapses, phases of struggle, dryness, and doubt. But these ought not to distress him unduly. Conscious feelings, however exalted, are not the only indications of spiritual progress.
>
> — *How to Know God: The Yoga Aphorisms of Patanjali,*
> 1981, by the Vedanta Society of Southern California

We may be growing most strongly at a time when our minds seem dark and dull. So we should never listen to the promptings of sloth, which will try to persuade us that this dullness is a sign of failure. There is no failure as long as we continue to make an effort.

The Jewish Psalter (the Psalms) is filled with deeply personal testimony on the issue of spiritual dryness and the surprising blessings often at its heart. The shocking cry from the Psalmist "My God, my God, why have you forsaken me" comes from Psalm 22:1. But the rest of the Psalm goes on eventually to describe a steadfast, growing faith in God's power to save and heal. The abandonment turns to blessing and deeper faith.

DEATH IS NOW

You are never going to be more dead than you are right now. Human life on Earth is a form of death. That's not just my opinion. It has been stated best by Professor Alvin Boyd Kuhn.

Dr. Kuhn, a prodigious researcher and linguist, was a believer in the ancient wisdom of the Egyptians, the Orphics, the Pythagoreans and Plato (there are also heavy echoes in Paul's letters) that said we are all "sparks of divine fire struck off from the flint of the Eternal," that is, immortal souls clad in mortal bodies. He expounded how in the minds of the earliest sages death meant life in the body now. That's where the Greek saying, that the body is the tomb of the soul—*soma sema*—originated. As we live our lives here, gaining experience and expanding consciousness, we are in a deep sense alienated from, or dead to, the spiritual realm whence we came ("trailing clouds of glory") and to which we shall return.

Here's the quote: "Right now, our deific souls are at the very bottom of the arc of death and can never be as dead again as they are now and have been." This understanding transforms the way most ancient texts should be read, including the many Books of the Dead. What we call death, the cessation of physical life on this plane, is the moment of our rebirthing and return to glory. Then, depending on how mature we have become spiritually through experience gained in our "death" in matter—our earthly existence—we either move on to "heaven" or the divine Presence (to take on new responsibilities) or must come back to what Paul calls "the body of this death" to reincarnate and grow further.

I am not certain yet about reincarnation, but some of the brightest of the early Christians believed in it—for example, Origen, and it was not until the sixth century that the church finally threw it out for the last time as heresy. The fact there was so much opposition to the idea from the authorities from the third century onwards leads one to suspect it was too much of a threat to the paternalism and authoritarianism that Rome had come to espouse so heartily. It didn't want people doing what Paul had commanded: "Work out your own salvation, with fear and trembling."

The ancient Chaldean Oracles said: "All things are the progeny of fire." That's what Kuhn's talking about. It's also what Plato was talking about. We come from the "fire" of the divine origin of everything that is, but most often we walk about in total forgetfulness of who we really are. "Humans on earth are like beings stricken with amnesia," says Plato. His whole doctrine of reminiscence (anamnesis), that is, that all learning is remembering what was already known but has been clouded by the weight of matter upon us, is based upon this thinking.

If what is being said here is true, and I am convinced it is so, then the function not just of education but of religion particularly is to impart lost memories of a former glory. Kuhn says it best: "Salvation, the whole aim of religion, is by way of rekindled memory of slumbering divinity." I love that! It certainly beats the attitude expressed in the Prayer of Humble Access, Book of Common Prayer: "We are not worthy . . . to gather up the crumbs under thy table but thy property is always to have mercy. . . ." by which we Anglicans attempted in the old Holy Communion service to crawl on our bellies back into the good graces of the Source of All Things.

Life in the body, according to the sages of old, is living "in the crucible of the great house of flame." Yes, life in this world can be beautiful—for some. But, hell, like death, is not some apocalyptic, otherworldly place; it is here and now. That's why all the ancient religions had at their centre a suffering deity. This was to represent the experience of every person born into this world—the experience of every soul in matter. It was also to manifest or dramatize the fact that the very act of Spirit entering the heart of matter at the dawn of creation itself was a form of divine "dying."

Even the Prometheus myth has this connection with the other crucified gods of antiquity and with the story of Jesus. Prometheus, the earliest mythical benefactor of humanity in its evolutionary struggle, was ". . . nailed by hands and feet, and with arms extended, to the rocks of Mount Caucasus." When one knows that this figure fastened to a cross or rock is but the outward dramatization of the truth of divine "impalement on the stake of matter," all overly historical realism associated with it, from crucifixes to lurid hymns about the "blood of the Lamb," becomes revolting and should be dropped.

GOD'S PERFECT LOVE
CASTS OUT CORROSIVE FEAR

To conquer fear is the beginning of wisdom.
— BERTRAND RUSSELL

Perfect love casts out fear.
— NEW TESTAMENT

———————————

Many think the Bible sees the greatest obstacle to human happiness as sin in one form or another. In fact, Christianity has been overly obsessed with sin and with our need for some outside redemption from it. A great deal of cruelty, guilt and misery have flowed as a result. I had known there was something distorted about this line of interpretation for many years, together with its doctrine of the total depravity of human beings—including newborn babies!—but I never got it into focus properly until one day I read a little book by the Scottish philosopher John Macmurray.

Macmurray, who became a Quaker because of the church's acceptance of war, said that when he first read the Gospels in an objective way, laying aside the dogma and teaching that had accumulated around them, he was amazed. He discovered that contrary to what he had been taught, the Gospel's Jesus' main preoccupation was not with sin at all. The attitude to sin was that it was to be repented of, forgiven, and let go—without need of clergy, rites or whatever. The real enemy of humankind, according to Jesus, was fear and its comrades—anxiety, worry and lack of trust.

Macmurray's words hit me like a lightning bolt and I couldn't wait to read the Four Gospels afresh for myself. Putting aside all I had learned in Sunday school, from thousands of sermons, from theological college and from libraries, I picked up my Greek New Testament (I was teaching Greek at the time at my old seminary) and began reading with new eyes. I quickly found that in the story, Jesus' most characteristic saying, his signature slogan, was "Be of good courage" or "Have confidence." He was always talking about the need for faith; faith, however, not in the sense of cerebral assent to certain creeds, propositions or other religiously correct opinions, but in the radical sense of a deep trust in life, the universe and the reality he called "Father." The thing that puzzled him most about both the disciples and the crowds was: "How is it that you have so little faith/trust?"

This entire experience had an enormous impact on my thinking about the Christian message. Two questions, nevertheless, remained: Is fear indeed the central problem for humanity, and, how is it to be dealt with? How can it be replaced by faith/confidence/trust?

Certainly nothing can rival fear when it comes to the corrosion of our inner poise, peace and happiness. There are obvious fears like the fear of a specific illness, fear of death, our own or that of our loved ones, fear of losing one's job, fear of failing at some task, fear of loneliness, fear of being afraid. But there are a thousand other subtle fears that plague us and rob us of tranquillity. And they can make us do things both strange and terrible.

Racism is ultimately based upon fear, fear of the unknown, fear of being diminished in some way or of losing out to strangers. The obscenity of militarism, unceasing production and sales of ever more deadly weaponry, and war itself are accompanied by greed, lust for power and a host of other evils, but the bottom line in the equation is one of fear—fear of one's neighbour, fear of not being number one, fear of loss of influence or of being taken over. At the root of most of the injustice responsible for the numbing suffering we witness daily in the news is fear. The fanatical fundamentalism evident today in so many regions of the world is the product of fear—fear of change, fear of uncertainty, fear of losing one's iden-tity, fear of thinking for oneself. We are living through a time when "men's hearts are failing them for fear."

Telling people bound by one or more deadly fears that they should simply relax and "be of good courage" or trust the universe is no help. It's a bit like advising someone caught in an acute depression to cheer up. Clearly, Jesus in the story did not engage in such folly. His confrontation with fear in his life was made possible through his overwhelming conviction that the Source of life itself could be trusted even unto and through death. And it was based upon Jesus' core spiritual experience, told, for example, in the symbolism of his baptism in Jordan where the story has him see the heavens open and hear a voice saying, "This is my beloved son." He was "filled by God's Spirit" as he became aware of being totally loved by "the Father" of all. It was his experience of a Presence at the heart of life and of being wholly loved by that Presence that gave him the assurance to conquer fear. That's the inner, mythic meaning of the story and it's aimed at us.

"Perfect love casts out fear." That doesn't mean our perfect love for God. Nobody has that. It's trusting God's perfect love for us that changes things. To the extent that we accept that, we can trust life, ourselves and each other. We can begin, perhaps haltingly at first, to let go and to say farewell to fear.

ONLY SUFFERING TRANSFORMS US

It is humanity's fate "to learn by suffering." In the classical Greek play *Agamemnon*, Aeschylus expresses this in three brief words—*tō pathei mathein*, but they contain a cosmic bite of spiritual wisdom.

This is the great theme at the heart of all the world's mythologies, from the epic of *Gilgamesh* and the *Odyssey* of Homer, to the Bhagavad-Gita. It's the central beat of all the heroic sagas of the past and the distilled essence of the Bible and most other sacred books. Look closely and you will find that it's also integral to the plotlines of most of the world's most magnificent novels and dramas.

This is the one truth that, complain, wriggle and squirm as we may, none of us can ultimately avoid. In a deep sense, it contains our individual destinies. It's how we respond to this key reality that determines who and what we become in life.

As the eminent French novelist Marcel Proust, who was himself a semi-invalid because of acute asthma, once put it: "Illness is the doctor to whom we pay most heed; to kindness, to knowledge, we make promises only; it is pain we obey."

Only a masochist seeks out pain or enjoys it. But pain and suffering get the immediate attention of all our faculties as nothing else can. As C. S. Lewis wrote in his book *The Problem of Pain*, "Pain plants the flag of truth in the fortress of a rebel heart."

Family, pleasure, work, service to others, the ongoing search for happiness—all of these occupy our time and bring us experiences that can enrich our lives enormously, but it is mental, emotional or physical suffering that snap us to attention and make us pay heed to more ultimate dimensions where true insight and soul-making are to be found. Flannery O'Connor wrote: "In a deep sense, sickness is a place more instructive than a long trip to Europe, and it's always a place where there's no company, where nobody can follow."

Many religious people have the very odd notion that somehow being devout or "saved" will spare them pain and sorrow; that their religion will provide an umbrella or a safety shield against all problems. This, of course, is nonsense. Indeed, the more serious the will to know and obey the divine within and without, the more certain is the price such discipleship will bring.

One of the reasons the Bible story of Jacob, the mother's boy who through trickery stole his brother Esau's birthright but then went on to tread the path of suffering and eventual transformation, is so compellingly powerful is that it bears eloquent witness to our theme. We are told allegorically that on the eve of a meeting with his brother, whom he feared, Jacob wrestled all night with an angel of the Lord. In one sense he prevailed, but he was injured in the struggle and was lame forever after.

In the film of Tolkien's *Return of the King*, Frodo's encounter with the monster spider, Shelob, left him with an enduring trauma from her bite. That pain was the price of great gain.

Commenting on this episode, the late Chuck Meyer, author of *Dying Church, Living God*, wrote:

> The angel knew what psychology would later discover, that people don't change unless there's enough pain or discomfort to do so. . . . So the wrestling will of necessity be painful for those of us who choose, reluctantly or otherwise, to engage God. The struggle will take as many forms as are useful to us, as many rounds as are required. It will take a lot to get our full attention, to jolt us from the distraction that our years of certainty about our identity (and God's) have created, and we will be permanently changed or injured before that still small voice whispers our true identity in our ears.

This is not easy. One reader put some of her struggle and pain in a letter. She said she has "gone through a dramatic change in thinking" from her traditional Catholic roots. She finds the idea of

God "sending his son only to Christians now seems foolish to me but there are so many beliefs I have to think through—and I don't want to throw out the baby with the bath water." While she finds her changed beliefs "make so much more sense," she admits to some pain of nostalgia too: "Sometimes I feel sad to have lost the 'security' of my past beliefs—it was black and white then and now I struggle to sort out what is truth and what isn't. It was much easier before!" There are so very many Christians and members of other faiths today who can deeply identify with that.

When I think of the people who have inspired me most, the heroes in every field of human endeavour, from politics to literature, they all have demonstrated from their lives the way in which hardships, obstacles and weaknesses of every kind have this latent, transfiguring potency to draw forth the very best that is in us. That's the reason that biographies and autobiographies can make such fascinating reading.

I once wrote a chapter called "The Weakness of an Apostle" for a book never published. It was about a side of Paul that seldom gets attention. No, I was not speculating about his "thorn in the flesh" but simply looking at his admissions of physical and emotional problems on a major scale. Nobody has done more to shape and promote a world religion than Paul. Few in religious history have been so open about their own frailties.

I could describe this in detail, but I'd prefer it if readers would read Paul's letters again themselves. The key to how he handled his problems lies in his famous words about how at the point when he was most weak, he became strong. God's strength—and wisdom—he found "is made perfect through weakness."

WE ARE ALL WEAK,
EVEN THOSE WHO STRAIN TO BE STRONG

According to popular wisdom, human beings are divided into two groups with an inevitability that almost amounts to divine predestination. There are only the strong and the weak. There are just winners and losers. Nobody in between. Since the vast majority want to be approved of, to fit in, and to appear to be making it, there's an enormous cultural pressure at least to seem to belong to the winners' caste. People knock themselves out to present the mask or persona of the strong. The cost of the strain and angst involved is often staggering. The resulting hypocrisy or lack of authenticity in living is endemic in our culture.

We need to re-examine this. There are not the strong and weak, but only the weak. All illusions about supermen and superwomen among us are just that—a deceptive mirage. There are only the weak, and this includes all those who are struggling to be seen as strong. The Swiss psychiatrist Paul Tournier wrote a book about this over twenty-five years ago. It was called simply *The Strong and the Weak*. He described, among other things, the healing and the power in the lives of those who come to realize their participation in the universal phenomenon of weakness. It's another way of saying that one has come to recognize his or her own true humanity. Jean Vanier keeps making the same point in his writing and his work with the physically and emotionally challenged.

Presently many people seem to be assuming the role of victim. The infantile urge to blame others and to shift responsibility for failure or chaos in one's life—or society in general—onto the shoulders of government, parents, institutional structures or specific traumas in one's past is completely counterproductive to inner growth.

Realizing our weakness has nothing to do with the victim complex. Rather, it's a matter of being honest about oneself and the overall human condition. There's a tremendous amount of wisdom in the ancient Greek proverb "Count no man happy until he's dead." In other words, it's the very nature of humanity to be instantly and always open to completely unforeseen ills, accidents or other misfortunes. And nobody, with the exception of God, has the slightest idea of what is really going on in the deepest thoughts and struggles of the person next to them at work or on the subway train or in the street.

One of the strongest men I have ever read about was Paul the Apostle. Had he not bared his soul to us in his letters, who would ever have guessed at his anxieties and weaknesses? There is also what he called his "thorn in the flesh"—most likely some physical ailment. His prayer that it be removed, repeated many times, received, he tells us, the answer no. Like all of us, Paul wanted magical or instant solutions to his problems. There was none. Instead, the deep answer of the cosmos, or "the Lord," was: "My grace is sufficient for thee: for my strength is made perfect in weakness."

If there was space here, one could take all the strong men and women of history and show this same phenomenon. They prevailed and fought the good fight not because they were perfect, had perfect parents, were born rich and gorgeous, or were free from struggles without and fears within. Their strength or success came from facing and wrestling with their human frailties to the very end. One can see this in the lives of so many great authors and artists; Beethoven springs to mind. One can also see it in Technicolor in the life and achievements of perhaps the strongest-seeming leader of this century, Sir Winston Churchill. Suffering all his life from bouts of manic depression, a devastating weakness, he nevertheless transcended it to become the very symbol and embodiment of courage and indomitable personal force against the greatest onslaught of evil in history.

By one of those great paradoxes which illumine the deeper wells of living, it's a mark of strength to face your weakness squarely. This is the very first step in any spiritual and moral growth. We need to assess carefully what our assets and liabilities are. Then, where changes are possible and desirable, our long life's work on ourselves can begin. There will be aspects of our innermost selves and of our humanity that cannot be changed but must be accepted as they are. If we become obsessed with the need to be in perfect health or perfect shape or to be or possess the perfect anything—from a perfect family to a perfect social image—we are doomed to endless frustration and a haunting sense of failure. Any doctor will tell you that nothing disturbs health and peace of mind like the illusion many hold that their life should be pain free and that every ache has a cure.

This is the real human story. There are no strong, only the weak. But it's the kind of response we give to the challenge of our human weakness that determines what kind of people and what kind of world we shall have. All the "strengths" of human achievement to this point have been won by transforming weakness into an advantage, into another opportunity to struggle and to grow. We need to tell that to ourselves. We need to tell it especially to our youth.

WILL THERE BE ANIMALS IN HEAVEN?

Will we one day be reunited with pets once loved and now no longer with us? For many people this is not a frivolous question. The human–animal bond is one of the most powerful forces in our earthly existence. Heaven, by which I mean the dimension or plane of being beyond physical death, would not be heaven for me if the rest of the animal kingdom were not to be included.

Some, of course, are scandalized on either intellectual or religious grounds by such hopes. There are those who doubt the possibility of life beyond the grave for any mortal being. Others, in a form of speciesism, hold that salvation pertains to humans only—and only a select few of them at that!

Both are wrong. We are wholly connected with other animals in the bundle of life and, believing as I do that there is more evidence for life after death than for total extinction, I'm convinced we will share our future with them.

Most religions hold to the ancient dogma that animals don't have souls, therefore, they're inferior in God's eyes. Contrary to what most people think, there is little clarity on this subject in the Bible. The prestigious *Oxford Dictionary of the Christian Church* begins its article on soul thus: "No precise teaching about the soul received general acceptance in the Christian Church until the Middle Ages. . . ."

However, the first and classic passage mentioning the human soul is in the second account of the creation of Adam or humankind in Genesis 2:7ff. (The other account of human creation is in Genesis 1:26.) In the King James Version, Genesis 2:7 reads: "And the Lord God formed man of the dust of the ground, and breathed into his nostrils the breath of life; and man became a living soul." The New Revised Standard Version says: ". . . and the man became a living being." The emphasis of this mythos or story in both translations is upon the idea not of "having" a soul, as one has an appendix, lungs or liver, but on "becoming" a living soul or being.

I believe the idea that we are souls—beings filled with the divine life force or energy that flows from God, capable of consciousness, purpose and love—means that we're part of a continuum of life including all other life forms. We're all part of a cosmic soul, an oversoul, as some describe it, sharing in it according to the development of all our capacities. We are human souls at varying stages of becoming; our pets are also souls. Can anyone truly look into the depths of the eyes of a beloved dog, cat, horse or any other animal and not feel kinship, love, loyalty and deep communication?

Like us, animals do not *have* souls. They *are* souls. They are made from the "dust of the Earth" as we are; they have, and are, distinct personalities with the breath of life and intelligence or consciousness within. They think and make decisions.

The myth of Genesis says that God not only created them, he blessed them, making them holy, and that he took pleasure in them. The story of the Flood and the ark, while not historical in the modern sense, carries the deep truth of the Eternal's concern for the whole of the created order.

In some of the most sublime passages in the entire Hebrew Bible, the text makes it clear that the biblical writers could not conceive of a new order of being at the end of the ages that does not include the creatures who share our common pilgrimage. Hosea speaks of a day when enmity between all forms of life will cease. Birds and snakes, for example, will no longer fear one another.

Isaiah exults that the wolf and the sheep will lie together, the leopard and goats will be at peace. Babies will not be harmed by deadly reptiles "and the lion shall eat straw like the ox." Similarly, even Paul, who was not much of a nature fan, says that all creatures await the day when God will resurrect his children. Animals and plants, caught up in the travails of this time plane, look forward expectantly (all creation stands on tiptoe, he says) to the age to come.

Just as pets and other animals have healing power over us here—the full extent of this is just now being rediscovered by researchers—so too will they be a part of our fuller healing and wholeness in the presence of God. Whales will leap and sing in oceans more pristine than at creation's dawn. Eagles will soar.

The "new heaven and Earth" of the age to come will be a time of the restoration of all things. The beauty, the companionship, the forgiveness and the love we have shared with other animals here "below" will shine with a fresh glory. Whatever heaven is, we've been promised that "all things" will be made new. The lion will lie down with the lamb. Every joyous relationship we have known on Earth with nature or with loved ones, human or not, will be restored and transcended.

So, to those who have ever mourned the loss of a pet or who have ever wondered wistfully whether the creatures who have given such joy in this life will be part of our future, there are plenty of grounds for comfort and for "a reasonable (i.e., rational) hope."

This being true, the ethical principles underlying our treatment of animals gain an entirely fresh perspective. If they indeed are souls, blessed by God and part of the ultimate schema of "eternal life," then how we behave towards them is as important as how we treat one another.

The ethic based upon the Golden Rule—not doing harm to anyone—is not meant to be understood only in a narrow, anthropic sense. It has profound implications for the relationship of humans to all creatures "great and small." It's an ethic for ecology as well as for all human societies.

People arguing against the existence of a loving God often use the fact that there is so much suffering in the animal kingdom as part of their case. The blunt fact, of course, is that by far the greatest suffering caused to animals is initiated by human beings alone.

The intimate closeness of the other animals to us and their involvement in our final destiny both here and hereafter is one

more potent reason for facing up to this evil and for determining to
do all in our power to ameliorate or eliminate it wherever we can.
For those who would like to read a full and hard-hitting discussion
of the ethics of a right relationship with the rest of the animals, I
recommend Peter Singer's *Animal Liberation*.

WE NEED OUR FAILURES

———————

My brother and I were once under our house looking at a water filter. I had asked George for his help since, besides being a doctor, he's also quite expert at fixing other things.

He showed me how to twist the seating for the filter in a way that shut off the water until a new one could be installed, and said, "You can buy a new filter at the hardware store and put it in yourself. You needn't call a plumber. It's no big deal."

How wrong he was! Next day, after he'd gone, I tackled the problem. It was much more than a "big deal"; it was a disaster in which I soaked myself to the skin and half flooded the place. Somehow the old filter came loose all right but the shut-off valve didn't work as it ought to have. Water under great pressure shot out in all directions. I struggled vainly to jam the thing back into place. Desperate, I yelled for Susan to come and bring a flashlight.

When she peered in and saw my predicament she was alarmed but not surprised. After the watery mess was finally brought under control, she reminded me of previous similar incidents where I had also been less than masterful. She suggested the time has come for me to accept the brute fact that as a plumber I'm a flop.

Failure is hard for anyone in our culture, especially males, to contemplate let alone accept. Our values and our rewards are pegged upon winners not losers. In my own religious upbringing, weakness and failure of any kind were viewed as ultimate taboos, signs of a lack of real faith or discipline—or of both.

Unfortunately, this kind of thinking permeates a lot of what poses as spirituality in our day. The cult of perfectionism, the idea that there is a "way" to gain complete control of oneself, others, or of life—some fail-safe regimen of praying, thinking, exercising, eating, meditating or whatever—is being touted and sold on every side. But though it brings some promoters dollars and fame, it remains a seductive lie.

We all walk with a limp. We're all wounded in varying degrees and ways. We're all going to fail and know weakness. It's an essential and indelible part of our humanity. There's a vast difference between trying to do one's best and succumbing to the notion that it's possible to be free of one's shadow, to be wholly above those "lesser mortals" who suffer from one form or other of emotional, physical or social flaw. There are no wholly strong, perfect human beings. As we have seen, there are only the weak and those who pretend not to be.

One of the things that rang true about the late Father Henri Nouwen, the reason for the great popularity of so many of his books, was that he saw with total clarity that any spirituality worthy of the name must be one that deals with this universal experience. He wrote openly of his own hurt. Unfortunately, though we lived only five or six kilometres apart, we never met. When he died suddenly last fall, he had just sent me his most recent book inscribed with: "Hoping we soon shall meet. Peace, Henri."

In a recent issue of the newsletter of the Jewish Association of Spiritual Healers based in New York City, an article called "The Spirituality of Imperfection" has this passage:

> Errors, of course, are part of the game, part of our truth as human beings. To deny our errors is to deny ourself for to be human is to be . . . somehow error-prone. The spirituality of imperfection speaks to those who seek meaning in the absurd, peace within the chaos, light within the darkness, joy within the suffering—without denying the reality and even the necessity of absurdity, chaos, darkness and suffering.
>
> This is not a spirituality for saints or gods but for people who suffer from what the psychologist William James called "torn-to-pieces-hood." The spirituality of imperfection speaks to both the inevitability of pain and to the possibility of healing within the pain.

This excerpt has echoes in it of the Psalms, of the Buddha, of Jesus and St. Paul. It belongs to the heart of any truly spiritual approach to life. Paradoxical though it is, the moment of success is rarely the moment of growth. As Jewish wisdom puts it: "The eye has a white and a dark part, but we can only see through the dark part. Through failure, we can begin to see. From darkness, comes insight. Given time and faith, such insight brings triumph."

IN EXILE FROM OUR TRUE HOME

Modern theologians with a progressive agenda like to make use of the metaphor of exile to describe themselves and the large body of Christians today who see and feel themselves cut off or alienated from their church. Their former or would-be leaders, their past theology and rituals, are regarded as almost wholly out of touch with who and where they believe they are.

The striking metaphor itself comes from the various exiles—some mythical, one or two probably historical—that are described in what Christians call the Old Testament, the Hebrew Bible. This theme of the Jews—"the people of God"—being forced into exile in foreign lands such as Babylonia, Persia, or wherever, runs vividly throughout the Scriptures.

When you reflect on it, however, the concept of being a captive stranger, or even an exiled king, in a strange land is a deeply archetypal construct in our own individual and collective unconscious. Like the other powerful religious archetypes in the human psyche, such as the god-man, dying and resurrecting divinities, virgin births, the sacred wise old man or woman, or the great mother, the motif of exile runs throughout the world's epic poetry, its folklore, ancient fairy tales and romantic fictions, from Homer, to Thomas Hardy, to the modern era and *Star Wars*.

The deeper roots of this "I-am-but-a-stranger-here" refrain have not been adequately explored by either the theologians or the creative writers who employ it so widely in their works. Colin Wilson, in his landmark book *The Outsider*, came close long ago, but only in a secular and partial manner.

Behind the notion of exile of which the Bible speaks on the surface, beneath the "exile" being written and spoken about by such critics of Christian orthodoxy as retired Episcopal bishop the Right Reverend John Spong, for example, when speaking of himself and the many who are sympathetic to his views, there lies a much more profound alienation or sense of dislocated otherness than the immediate reference denotes.

In a radical manner as a race, or rather as a species, we are each of us in exile from our own true home. Like the Prodigal Son in the parable in Luke, we are all "in a far country" together. As Wordsworth so movingly wrote in *Intimations of Immortality*, we do not originate from here, nor is this Earth our final destination:

> *The Soul that rises with us, our life's star,*
> *Hath had elsewhere its setting,*
> *And cometh from afar:*
> *Not in entire forgetfulness,*
> *And not in utter nakedness,*
> *But trailing clouds of glory do we come*
> *From God, who is our home.*

Is it any wonder, then, that we humans are so often filled with such a "divine discontent"? Is it that unusual that at times we are overtaken by inexplicable moods or feelings that, in spite of all its joys and miracles and beauty, this world is somehow not enough, that our true country or place of belonging lies somehow somewhere else? Perhaps it may be a familiar scent, a certain sound, a haunting melody, a suddenly remembered voice or a glimpse of landscape, and it seems that in it we see or hear echoes of our true native "land."

These "intimations of immortality," as Wordsworth called them, are to me signs and hints of the real universality of the Christian doctrine of the Incarnation. Remember always: We are all of us Incarnations of the word made flesh. We are all bearers of Christ-consciousness within, and need to claim this inheritance for ourselves.

We are here to gain experience, to grow, to learn, to serve others, to add to God's knowledge and experience of his/her own vast potentialities, but one day, deep down, we know we are going to be truly going home. The days of our exile as flesh-embodied spirits here will be over and our tasks done. And then, as T. S. Eliot said, "All shall be well and all manner of thing shall be well."